MEDITERRANEAN DIET COOKBOOK WITH PICTURES

Start Your Mediterranean Journey with Mouthwatering Recipes and Beginner Tips for Success

Samuel Witte

TABLE OF CONTENTS

INTRODUCTION TO THE MEDITERRANEAN DIET

The Mediterranean Diet represents an eating approach inspired by the customary nutritional practices of the Mediterranean region. This diet is characterized by abundant fresh fruits and vegetables, whole grains, legumes, seeds and nuts, and healthy fats such as olive oil. It is also low in red meat and dairy and includes moderate fish, poultry, and wine.

The Mediterranean Diet, which has been thoroughly studied, boasts many health advantages, such as lowering the likelihood of heart disease, stroke, and specific cancer types, enhancing cognitive abilities, and promoting a longer life. It is also a delicious and satisfying eating method that is easy to follow and adapt to your taste and lifestyle.

The Mediterranean Diet is an excellent choice whether you want to improve your health, lose weight, or try something new. This cookbook is designed to help you start your Mediterranean Diet journey with simple and delicious recipes that are easy to prepare and packed with the healthy ingredients that are the cornerstone of this way of eating. So, let's dive into Mediterranean cuisine and discover the many benefits of this delicious and healthy way of life!

The Mediterranean diet is commonly regarded as among the world's most nutritious eating plans, and this perception is well-founded. This dietary pattern is based on the traditional foods consumed by people living in the Mediterranean region, including Italy, Greece, and Spain. This diet is marked by its focus on the whole, minimally processed food items, including fruits, vegetables, whole grains, legumes, and healthful fats like olive oil.

In addition to being delicious, the Mediterranean diet has numerous health benefits. Studies have demonstrated that this diet can aid in lowering the likelihood of developing heart disease, stroke, type 2 diabetes, and specific cancer types. It can also improve brain function, boost longevity, and promote a healthy weight.

A significant factor in the Mediterranean diet's effectiveness is its emphasis on moderation and equilibrium. Instead of eliminating whole food categories or tracking caloric intake, the Mediterranean diet promotes consuming various foods in moderation and relishing every mouthful. This makes it a sustainable and enjoyable way of eating rather than a restrictive diet that is difficult to stick to.

Regardless of being a novice or an experienced individual, this Mediterranean diet recipe book offers the resources necessary to integrate this wholesome dietary approach into your daily routine. This recipe book contains everything from savory dishes to helpful advice and techniques to enhance your Mediterranean diet experience. So why wait? Embark on the path towards improved health and increased happiness today!

Definition Of the Mediterranean Diet

The Mediterranean Diet is based on the idea that food should be enjoyed and consumed in moderation and that meals should be shared and savored with family and friends. This way of eating has been linked to several health benefits, including lower rates of heart disease, obesity, and certain types of cancer.

In addition to emphasizing healthy food choices, the Mediterranean Diet incorporates physical activity and a relaxed, stress-free lifestyle. This holistic approach to health and wellness has made the Mediterranean Diet one of the world's most popular and well-researched diets.

The Mediterranean Diet represents an eating approach grounded in the customary eating habits of nations bordering the Mediterranean Sea. High consumption of fruits and vegetables, whole grains, legumes, nuts, moderate amounts of fish and poultry, and limited amounts of dairy products, red meat, and sweets characterizes this diet. The diet also includes healthy fats, such as olive oil and moderate wine.

A distinguishing characteristic of the Mediterranean Diet is the focus on plant-derived food sources, which are abundant in fiber, vitamins, and minerals, along with heart-beneficial monounsaturated and polyunsaturated fats. This eating approach has been linked to numerous health advantages, such as a decreased likelihood of heart disease, stroke, and specific cancer types, enhanced cognitive function, weight control, and increased life expectancy.

In addition to the specific foods included in the Mediterranean Diet, how these foods are prepared and consumed is also important. Meals are typically enjoyed in a relaxed setting, with family and friends, and without the distractions of electronic devices. This social aspect of the diet has been shown to positively impact overall well-being and be an essential component of a healthy lifestyle.

In general, the Mediterranean Diet is a well-rounded, whole-food-focused eating style that has been appreciated for centuries by those in the Mediterranean area and is now being adopted globally as a nutritious and tasty food option.

Health Benefits of The Mediterranean Diet

The Mediterranean diet is not just a way of eating but also a lifestyle proven to have numerous health benefits. This way of eating is centered around consuming whole, minimally processed foods, emphasizing plant-based foods, and incorporating moderate amounts of healthy fats and proteins. The following are some of the critical health benefits associated with following a Mediterranean diet:

- Bolster's heart health: The Mediterranean diet lowers the likelihood of heart disease, stroke, and elevated blood pressure. This results from the diet's focus on ingesting beneficial fats, like olive oil, while restricting detrimental fats, like saturated and trans fats.
- Aids in sustaining a healthy weight: The diet is abundant in fiber, contributing to a feeling of fullness and satisfaction, which decreases the chances of excessive eating and supports weight reduction. Additionally, the high intake of fruits, vegetables, and whole grains helps to provide a low-calorie, nutrient-dense diet.
- Lowers risk of chronic diseases: The Mediterranean diet has been associated with a decreased likelihood of developing chronic illnesses, including type 2 diabetes, specific cancers, and Alzheimer's disease. This is due to the diet's emphasis on consuming nutrient-dense, whole foods high in antioxidants and other beneficial compounds.
- Supports healthy aging: Research indicates that adhering to a Mediterranean diet can contribute to healthy aging by lowering the chances of diseases associated with aging and fostering sound cognitive performance.
- Improves mental health: The Mediterranean diet has been linked to improved mental health and a reduced risk of depression. This is thought to result from the significant consumption of beneficial fats, like omega-3 fatty acids, and the limited intake of detrimental fats.

The Mediterranean diet is a healthy, balanced eating method with numerous health benefits. By focusing on whole, minimally processed foods and incorporating healthy fats and proteins, this way of eating can help to promote overall health and well-being.

Fundamental Principles of The Mediterranean Diet

The Mediterranean Diet is a set of specific foods and ways of life emphasizing healthy and balanced eating.

Here are the fundamental principles of the Mediterranean Diet:

1. Emphasizes whole, natural foods: The Mediterranean Diet focuses on unprocessed, natural food items like fruits, vegetables, whole grains, legumes, nuts, seeds, and healthful oils such as olive oil. Processed and refined foods are limited.
2. Includes healthy fats: Olive oil is a staple in the Mediterranean Diet and is used in cooking and as a salad dressing. Nuts and seeds are also consumed for their healthy fat content.
3. Moderate protein intake: The Mediterranean Diet includes moderate amounts of lean protein sources such as fish, poultry, and legumes. Red meat is limited to a few times per month.
4. Restrained dairy: The Mediterranean Diet incorporates modest quantities of dairy products like cheese and yogurt, with a preference for low-fat choices.
5. Incorporates herbs and spices: The Mediterranean Diet incorporates a variety of herbs and spices to flavor foods, reducing the need for added salt and sugar.
6. Includes moderate wine consumption: red wine is consumed moderately within a well-rounded diet, underscoring the importance of temperance.

By following these fundamental principles, the Mediterranean Diet provides a balanced approach to eating that is both delicious and nutritious.

Foods To Include and Foods to Avoid

A plethora of unprocessed, natural foods like fruits, vegetables, whole grains, nuts, seeds, and healthy fats such as olive oil marks the Mediterranean diet. In addition, it highlights lean proteins l Foods to Include:

- Fruits: Fresh or dried fruits, such as grapes, oranges, lemons, and figs, are essential to the Mediterranean diet.
- Vegetables: Various fresh, colorful vegetables, such as tomatoes, zucchini, eggplant, bell peppers, and spinach, are a cornerstone of this way of eating.

- Whole Grains: Whole grain products like whole wheat bread, brown rice, and quinoa are crucial carbohydrates in the Mediterranean diet.
- Legumes: Beans, lentils, and chickpeas are an essential source of plant-based protein and fiber in the Mediterranean diet.
- Seeds and Nuts: Nuts and seeds like almonds, walnuts, and sunflower seeds are a great source of healthy fats, fiber, and protein in the Mediterranean diet.
- Healthy Fats: Olive oil is the primary source of healthy fats in the Mediterranean diet and is used for cooking and dressing.
- Fish and Seafood: Fish, such as salmon, mackerel, and sardines, are an essential source of omega-3 fatty acids in the Mediterranean diet.
- Poultry: Chicken or turkey can be incorporated into the Mediterranean diet in moderation.
- Dairy: Low-fat dairy products such as yogurt and cheese can be included in the Mediterranean diet but in moderation.
- Eggs: In moderation, eggs can be a flexible food item that fits well into the Mediterranean diet.
- Red Meat: Red meat is consumed in small quantities in the Mediterranean diet, typically lean beef or pork cuts.

Foods to Avoid:

- Processed Foods: The Mediterranean diet should limit processed foods with added sugars, refined carbohydrates, and unhealthy fats.
- Fried Foods: French fries should be avoided in the Mediterranean diet.
- High-Fat Meats: The Mediterranean diet should limit high-fat meats such as bacon, sausage, and deli.
- Sweets and Desserts: Sweets and desserts, such as cakes, cookies, and candy, should be limited to the Mediterranean diet.
- Alcohol: Alcohol should be consumed in moderation in the Mediterranean diet, with a preference for red wine.

Adhering to these recommendations ensures your meals adhere to the Mediterranean diet's core principles and allows you to enjoy its numerous health advantages.

Meal Planning and Recipe Ideas

Now that you understand the fundamental principles and foods of the Mediterranean Diet, it's time to put it into action. Meal planning is crucial to adopting any new diet, and the Mediterranean Diet is no exception. In this chapter, we will provide some tips and tricks for meal planning and a collection of delicious and easy-to-prepare recipes to help get you started.

When devising meal plans, it is crucial to remember the Mediterranean Diet's basic tenets, which involve integrating an abundance of fruits, vegetables, whole grains, and healthful fats into your diet. In addition, limiting your consumption of processed foods and red meat is also essential.

Consider planning your meals for the week in advance to make meal planning easier. This approach aids in maintaining organization and guarantees the consistent availability of nutritious components. You can also consider preparing some ingredients, such as chopping vegetables or cooking grains, to make meal preparation faster and more efficient.

Remember, the Mediterranean Diet is not about strict rules or deprivation but about incorporating healthy, flavorful foods into your meals to create a balanced and satisfying diet. So, let's get cooking!

The Mediterranean Diet focuses on food choices and eating habits, emphasizing shared meals with loved ones, relishing every mouthful, and appreciating the tastes and scents of the cuisine. Meal planning is an integral part of following the Mediterranean Diet, as it helps you stay on track and ensure a balanced and nutritious diet.

These recipes will help you understand the key ingredients and flavors of the Mediterranean Diet and show you how to create satisfying and healthy meals.

Some examples of meals that you can include in your meal planning are:

- Breakfast: Whole grain toast with avocado and egg, Greek yogurt with fresh fruit and honey, or a vegetable omelet
- Lunch: Grilled chicken or fish with a mixed greens salad, a quinoa and vegetable bowl, or a hummus and vegetable wrap
- Dinner: Grilled salmon with roasted vegetables, a vegetable and bean stew, or a pasta dish with a tomato-based sauce and plenty of fresh herbs.

In addition to these meal ideas, we will provide recipes for snacks, soups, and desserts that align with the Mediterranean Diet principles. So get ready to start your culinary journey and discover the delicious and healthy world of the Mediterranean Diet!

BREAKFAST RECIPES

MEDITERRANEAN BREAKFAST FRITTATA WITH TOMATOES, FETA, AND SPINACH

Preparation Time: 10 minutes

Cook Time: 20 minutes

Servings: 4

Ingredients:

- 8 large eggs
- 1/4 cup milk
- 1/4 teaspoon salt
- 1/4 teaspoon black pepper
- 1 tablespoon olive oil
- 1 cup cherry tomatoes, halved
- 1 cup fresh spinach, chopped
- 1/2 cup crumbled feta cheese
- 2 tablespoons chopped fresh basil

Instructions:

1. Whisk the eggs, milk, salt, and pepper in a large mixing bowl until well combined.

2. In a 10-inch nonstick skillet, heat the olive oil over medium heat. Add the cherry tomatoes and cook for 2-3 minutes, until they soften.
3. Incorporate the diced spinach into the frying pan and sauté for approximately 2 minutes until it begins to wilt.
4. Pour the combined eggs into the skillet and cook for roughly 5 minutes until the border begins to solidify.
5. Sprinkle the feta cheese and chopped basil on top of the frittata.
6. Place the skillet into the oven and broil for 3-5 minutes, until the frittata's center is firm and the cheese has melted and acquired a golden hue.
7. Slice the frittata into triangular portions and serve while still hot.

Nutrition Information per serving:
Calories: 196 Fat: 14 g Saturated Fat: 5 g Cholesterol: 372 mg Sodium: 607 mg Carbohydrates: 4 g Fiber: 1 g Protein: 16 g

MEDITERRANEAN-INSPIRED SHAKSHUKA

Preparation time: 10 minutes

Cook time: 20 minutes

Servings: 2

Ingredients:

- 1 tablespoon olive oil
- 1 red onion, chopped
- 2 cloves garlic, minced
- 1 red bell pepper, chopped
- 1 teaspoon cumin
- 1 teaspoon paprika
- 1 can of diced tomatoes
- 4 large eggs
- Salt and pepper to taste
- 1 tablespoon fresh parsley, chopped
- 2 slices of whole-grain bread

Instructions:

1. Warm up the olive oil in a sizable frying pan over medium heat.
2. Add the chopped onion, garlic, and red bell pepper and cook until soft and translucent, about 5 minutes.
3. Stir in the cumin and paprika, and cook for another minute.
4. Add the canned tomatoes to the skillet and let it simmer for 10 minutes.
5. Using a spoon, create four wells in the tomato mixture.
6. Gently break one egg into each space and sprinkle with salt and pepper.
7. Put a lid over the skillet and allow the eggs to cook until the egg whites have become firm while the yolks remain soft and runny, for approximately 5-7 minutes.
8. Serve the shakshuka with fresh parsley and whole-grain bread.

Nutrition Information (per serving):

Calories: 334 Fat: 22g Carbohydrates: 20g Protein: 14g Fiber: 5g Sugar: 8g

MEDITERRANEAN SHAKSHUKA WITH FETA

Preparation time: 10 minutes Cook time: 15 minutes Servings: 4

Ingredients:

- 4 large eggs
- 1 large tomato, chopped
- 1 medium red pepper, chopped
- 1 medium onion, chopped
- 2 garlic cloves, minced
- 1 teaspoon paprika
- 1 teaspoon cumin
- Salt and pepper, to taste
- 1 tablespoon olive oil
- 1/4 cup crumbled feta cheese
- Fresh parsley, chopped (optional, for garnish)

Instructions:

1. In a large skillet over medium heat, heat the olive oil. Add the onion, red pepper, and garlic and cook until the vegetables are soft about 5 minutes.
2. Stir in the paprika, cumin, salt, and pepper, and cook for another minute.
3. Add the chopped tomatoes to the skillet and cook until they are soft about 5 minutes.
4. Using a spoon, make 4 wells in the tomato mixture. Crack an egg into each well.
5. Cover the skillet and cook until the eggs are set to your desired level of doneness, about 5 minutes.
6. Sprinkle the feta cheese over the shakshuka and garnish with fresh parsley, if desired.
7. Serve with toasted bread or pita for dipping into the shakshuka.

MEDITERRANEAN-STYLE FRITTATA WITH TOMATOES AND FETA

Preparation Time: 10 minutes
Cook Time: 20 minutes
Servings: 4

Ingredients:

- 6 large eggs
- 1/4 cup milk
- Salt and pepper, to taste
- 1 tablespoon olive oil
- 1 medium onion, chopped
- 2 medium tomatoes, chopped
- 1/4 cup crumbled feta cheese
- 2 tablespoons chopped fresh basil

Instructions:

1. Whisk the eggs, milk, salt, and pepper in a large bowl. Set aside.

2. Heat olive oil in a large oven-safe frying pan over medium heat. Please put in the onion and sauté until it softens and turns translucent roughly 5 minutes.
3. Add the chopped tomatoes to the skillet and cook for 2 minutes.
4. Empty the egg mixture into the skillet with the vegetables. Let it cook for around 3-5 minutes until the border starts to solidify.
5. Sprinkle the feta cheese on top of the frittata and place the skillet in the oven.
6. Bake at 400°F for 10-12 minutes until the frittata is set and lightly browned on top.
7. After allowing it to cool briefly, cut the dish into sections and garnish it with fresh basil.

Nutrition Info (per serving):
Calories: 168 Fat: 12 g Carbs: 6 g Protein: 12 g

SPINACH, FETA, AND TOMATO OMELET

Preparation time: 10 minutes
Cook time: 10 minutes
Servings: 1

Ingredients:

- 2 large eggs
- 2 tablespoons milk
- Salt and pepper, to taste
- 1 tablespoon olive oil
- 1 cup fresh spinach leaves
- 1/4 cup crumbled feta cheese
- 1/4 cup diced tomatoes
- Fresh basil leaves, for garnish (optional)

Instructions:

1. Whisk the eggs, milk, salt, and pepper in a medium bowl.

2. Over medium heat, warm up the olive oil in a non-stick frying pan.
3. Add the spinach leaves and cook until wilted about 2 minutes.
4. Pour the egg mixture into the skillet, swirling to distribute the spinach evenly.
5. Sprinkle the feta cheese and diced tomatoes over one-half of the omelet.
6. Use a spatula to gently fold the other half of the omelet over the filling.
7. Cook until the eggs are set and the cheese is melted about 5 minutes.
8. If desired, slide the omelet onto a plate and garnish with fresh basil leaves.
9. Serve hot, and enjoy!

Nutrition information (per serving):
Calories: 327 Fat: 25g Carbohydrates: 7g Protein: 18g

MEDITERRANEAN BREAKFAST BOWL

Preparation time: 10 minutes

Cook time: 10 minutes

Servings: 1

Ingredients:

- 1 cup cooked quinoa
- 1/2 cup chopped cherry tomatoes
- 1/4 cup sliced Kalamata olives
- 1/4 cup crumbled feta cheese
- 1/4 cup chopped cucumber
- 1 tbsp. freshly squeezed lemon juice
- 1 tbsp. extra-virgin olive oil
- Salt and pepper, to taste
- 1 fried egg (optional)

Instructions:

1. Combine the cooked quinoa, cherry tomatoes, Kalamata olives, feta cheese, and cucumber in a bowl.
2. In a separate bowl, whisk together the lemon juice and olive oil. Season with salt and pepper.
3. Add the dressing to the quinoa mixture and blend everything.
4. Optional: top the bowl with a fried egg.
5. Serve immediately and enjoy your Mediterranean breakfast bowl!

Nutrition Info (per serving):

Calories: 450 Fat: 28 g Carbohydrates: 39 g Protein: 14 g Sodium: 730 mg Sugar: 3 g

MEDITERRANEAN BREAKFAST FRITTATA

Preparation Time: 10 minutes
Cook Time: 25 minutes
Servings: 4

Ingredients:

- 8 large eggs
- 1/4 cup milk
- Salt and pepper, to taste
- 1 tablespoon olive oil
- 1 small red onion, chopped
- 1 red bell pepper, chopped
- 1 cup cherry tomatoes, halved
- 1/2 cup crumbled feta cheese
- 1/4 cup chopped fresh basil

Instructions:

1. Preheat the oven to 375°F.
2. Whisk the eggs, milk, salt, and pepper in a large bowl.
3. In a large oven-safe skillet, heat the olive oil over medium heat.

4. Add the red onion, bell pepper, and cherry tomatoes to the skillet and cook until the vegetables are tender about 5 minutes.
5. Empty the egg mixture into the vegetable-filled skillet and sprinkle some feta cheese.
6. Cook until the edges are set and the center is slightly runny about 5 minutes.
7. Transfer the skillet to the oven and bake for 10-15 minutes or until the frittata is fully cooked and golden brown on top.
8. Garnish with fresh basil and serve warm.

Nutrition Information (per serving):
Calories: 234 Fat: 19 g Carbohydrates: 6 g Protein: 14 g Sodium: 564 mg

MEDITERRANEAN SCRAMBLED EGGS WITH SPINACH AND FETA

Preparation Time: 5 minutes
Cook Time: 10 minutes
Servings: 2

Ingredients:

- 4 large eggs
- 2 tablespoons milk
- Salt and pepper, to taste
- 1 tablespoon olive oil
- 1 cup fresh spinach leaves
- 1/4 cup crumbled feta cheese
- 2 slices of whole grain bread, toasted

Instructions:

1. Whisk the eggs, milk, salt, and pepper in a medium bowl.
2. Warm up the olive oil over medium heat in a moderate-sized frying pan.

3. Put the spinach into the pan and cook until it wilts, which usually takes around 2 minutes.
4. Pour the egg mixture into the pan with the spinach and scramble until fully cooked, about 5 minutes.
5. Add the feta cheese to the mixture and cook for another minute while stirring.
6. Serve the scrambled eggs on top of the toasted whole-grain bread.

Nutrition Information (per serving):

Calories: 165 Total Fat: 12g Saturated Fat: 4g Cholesterol: 372mg Sodium: 474mg Total Carbohydrates: 4g Dietary Fiber: 2g Sugars: 2g Protein: 13g

MEDITERRANEAN VEGGIE AND FETA OMELETTE

Preparation Time: 10 minutes
Cook Time: 10 minutes
Servings: 1

Ingredients:

- 2 large eggs
- 1/4 cup diced red bell pepper
- 1/4 cup diced onion
- 1/4 cup diced cherry tomatoes
- 2 tablespoons crumbled feta cheese
- 1 tablespoon chopped fresh basil
- Salt and pepper, to taste
- 1 teaspoon extra-virgin olive oil

Instructions:

1. In a bowl, whisk together the eggs and season with salt and pepper.
2. Place the olive oil into a non-stick skillet over medium heat. Once hot, add the red bell pepper and onion and cook until soft, about 3-4 minutes.
3. Incorporate the cherry tomatoes and cook for an additional 1-2 minutes.
4. Pour the egg mixture into the skillet and cook until set, about 2-3 minutes.
5. Sprinkle the feta cheese and chopped basil on one half of the omelet.
6. Use a spatula to fold the other half of the omelet over the feta and basil.
7. Cook for another minute until the cheese is melted.
8. Serve hot.

Nutrition Information (per serving):

Calories: 245 Fat: 18g Saturated Fat: 6g Cholesterol: 373mg Sodium: 420mg Carbohydrates: 8g Fiber: 2g Protein: 16g

MEDITERRANEAN YOGURT PARFAIT WITH FRESH BERRIES AND ALMONDS

Preparation time: 10 minutes
Cook time: None
Servings: 1

Ingredients:

- 1 cup plain Greek yogurt
- 1/2 cup mixed fresh berries (such as strawberries, blueberries, and raspberries)
- 2 tablespoons chopped almonds
- 1 teaspoon honey

Instructions:

1. Blend the Greek yogurt and honey in a sizable bowl until thoroughly combined. In a separate bowl, mix the mixed berries.

2. Layer the yogurt mixture, mixed berries, and chopped almonds in a large glass or serving dish.
3. Repeat the layering until all ingredients are used up.
4. Serve immediately, garnished with additional almonds and honey if desired.

Nutrition Information (per serving):
Calories: 346 Fat: 18 g Saturated Fat: 3 g Cholesterol: 9 mg Sodium: 87 mg Carbohydrates: 33 g Fiber: 4 g Sugar: 25 g Protein: 18 g

MEDITERRANEAN-STYLE YOGURT BOWL WITH FRESH BERRIES AND NUTS

Preparation Time: 10 minutes Cook
Time: 0 minutes
Servings: 1

Ingredients:

- 1 cup plain Greek yogurt
- 1/2 cup mixed fresh berries (strawberries, blueberries, blackberries, raspberries)
- 1 tablespoon chopped mixed nuts (almonds, walnuts, pecans)
- 1 tablespoon honey
- 1 teaspoon lemon zest

Instructions:

1. Mix Greek yogurt, berries, nuts, honey, and lemon zest in a bowl.
2. Serve in a bowl and enjoy!

Nutrition Information (per serving):

Calories: 400 Protein: 24g Fat: 22g Carbohydrates: 38g Fiber: 5g Sugar: 28g

MEDITERRANEAN BREAKFAST WRAP WITH HUMMUS AND VEGGIES

Preparation Time: 10 minutes Cook Time: 5 minutes Servings: 1

Ingredients:

- 1 large whole-grain tortilla
- 2 tablespoons hummus
- 1/2 red bell pepper, sliced
- 1/2 yellow onion, sliced
- 1/2 cup baby spinach
- 1 egg, beaten
- Salt and pepper, to taste
- 1 tablespoon crumbled feta cheese
- 1 tablespoon chopped fresh parsley (optional)

Instructions:

1. Warm up a large non-stick pan over medium heat.
2. Spread the hummus evenly over the tortilla.

3. Place the sliced red bell pepper and yellow onion on half the tortilla.
4. Top the veggies with the baby spinach.
5. In the same pan, scramble the beaten egg until cooked through.
6. Spoon the scrambled egg over the veggies on the tortilla.
7. Sprinkle with salt, pepper, and crumbled feta cheese.
8. Fold the tortilla in half, enclosing the fillings.
9. Cook the wrap in the pan for approximately 2-3 minutes until the tortilla has turned crispy and the cheese has melted.
10. Serve with a sprinkle of chopped fresh parsley, if desired.

Nutrition Information (per serving):
Calories: 425 Total Fat: 25g Saturated Fat: 8g Cholesterol: 220mg Sodium: 730mg
Total Carbohydrates: 34g Dietary Fiber: 7g Sugars: 5g Protein: 19g

MEDITERRANEAN YOGURT PARFAIT

Preparation time: 10 minutes
Cook time: 0 minutes
Servings: 1

Ingredients:

- 1 cup Greek yogurt
- 1/2 cup mixed berries (such as strawberries, blueberries, and raspberries)
- 2 tbsp diced nuts (like almonds or walnuts)
- 1 tablespoon honey
- 1 teaspoon lemon zest
- 1/4 teaspoon vanilla extract

Instructions:

1. Mix the yogurt, lemon zest, and vanilla extract in a bowl.
2. In a separate bowl, mix the mixed berries.
3. Layer the yogurt mixture and the mixed berry mixture in a serving glass.

4. Sprinkle diced nuts on top and drizzle with honey.
5. Serve right away and relish in your delectable and nutritious Mediterranean yogurt parfait!

Nutrition Information (per serving):

Calories: 350 Fat: 15g Carbohydrates: 41g Protein: 17g Sodium: 95mg Fiber: 4g

MEDITERRANEAN-STYLE AVOCADO TOAST WITH FRIED EGGS

Preparation Time: 10 minutes
Cook Time: 10 minutes
Servings: 2

Ingredients:

- 2 slices of whole-grain bread
- 1 ripe avocado, pitted and mashed
- 1 lemon, juiced
- Salt and pepper, to taste
- 2 large eggs
- 2 tablespoons olive oil
- 1 tomato, diced
- 2 tablespoons crumbled feta cheese
- Fresh basil leaves, chopped, for garnish

Instructions:

1. Toast the bread slices until golden brown.

2. Mix the mashed avocado, lemon juice, salt, and pepper in a small bowl.
3. Distribute the avocado mixture evenly onto each slice of toast.
4. In a small non-stick pan, heat the olive oil over medium heat.
5. Break the eggs into the pan and cook until the egg whites have set but the yolks are still soft and runny, typically taking around 3-4 minutes.
6. Place a fried egg on top of each slice of avocado toast.
7. Top with diced tomato, crumbled feta cheese, and chopped basil leaves.
8. Serve immediately and enjoy your Mediterranean-style avocado toast with fried eggs.

Nutrition Information (per serving):
Calories: 470 Fat: 37g Saturated Fat: 9g Cholesterol: 186mg Sodium: 310mg Carbohydrates: 26g Fiber: 9g Sugar: 4g Protein: 14g

GREEK YOGURT PARFAIT WITH FRESH BERRIES AND HONEY

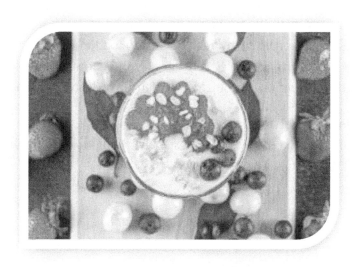

Preparation Time: 10 minutes
Cook Time: None
Servings: 1

Ingredients:

- 1 cup plain Greek yogurt
- 1/2 cup mixed fresh berries (strawberries, blueberries, raspberries)
- 1 tbsp honey
- 1 tbsp chopped almonds

Instructions:

1. In a clear glass or bowl, layer half of the Greek yogurt.
2. Top with half of the mixed berries.
3. Drizzle with half of the honey.
4. Repeat with remaining ingredients.
5. Sprinkle with chopped almonds.
6. Serve immediately.

Nutrition Information (per serving):

Calories: 300 Fat: 9g Saturated Fat: 1.5g Cholesterol: 15mg Sodium: 125mg Carbohydrates: 39g Fiber: 3g Sugar: 31g Protein: 20g

MEDITERRANEAN OATMEAL BOWL WITH FRESH BERRIES AND ALMONDS

Preparation time: 5 minutes

Cook time: 10 minutes

Servings: 1

Ingredients:

- 1/2 cup rolled oats
- 1 cup almond milk
- 1/2 teaspoon ground cinnamon
- 1/4 teaspoon vanilla extract
- 1/4 cup fresh berries (strawberries, blueberries, or raspberries)
- 2 tablespoons chopped almonds
- 1 tablespoon honey
- 1 tablespoon chia seeds

Instructions:

1. Bring the almond milk, oats, and cinnamon to a boil in a medium saucepan.
2. Lower the heat to low and cook for approximately 5-7 minutes or until the oats have absorbed most of the liquid.
3. Stir in the vanilla extract and chia seeds, and continue cooking for another 2-3 minutes.
4. Move the oatmeal to a bowl and garnish it with fresh berries, diced almonds, and a small amount of honey. Serve and enjoy!

Nutrition Information (per serving):

Calories: 378 Fat: 14g Carbohydrates: 54g Protein: 12g Sugar: 23g Fiber: 10g

MEDITERRANEAN-STYLE OATMEAL WITH ALMONDS, BERRIES, AND HONEY

Preparation Time: 5 minutes
Cook Time: 5 minutes
Servings: 2

Ingredients:

- 1 cup old-fashioned oats
- 2 cups almond milk
- 1/2 teaspoon ground cinnamon
- 1/4 teaspoon ground nutmeg
- 1/4 teaspoon ground allspice
- 1/4 teaspoon salt
- 1/2 cup mixed berries (such as blueberries, raspberries, and blackberries)
- 1/4 cup slivered almonds
- 2 tablespoons honey
- 2 tablespoons chopped fresh mint (optional)

Instructions:
1. Combine the oats, almond milk, cinnamon, nutmeg, allspice, and salt in a medium saucepan and bring them to a boil over medium heat.
2. Reduce the heat to low and let the oatmeal simmer for 5 minutes, occasionally stirring, until it is thick and creamy.
3. Remove the oatmeal from the heat and divide it into two bowls.
4. If using, top each bowl of oatmeal with half of the mixed berries, slivered almonds, honey, and fresh mint.

Nutrition Information (per serving):
Calories: 380 Fat: 16g Saturated Fat: 1g Cholesterol: 0mg Sodium: 260mg Carbohydrates: 52g
Fiber: 8g Sugar: 23g Protein: 12g

MEDITERRANEAN BREAKFAST SALAD WITH GRILLED HALLOUMI

Preparation Time: 10 minutes

Cook Time: 5 minutes

Servings: 4

Ingredients:

- 2 cups of mixed greens
- 1 cup of cherry tomatoes, halved
- 1 cup of cucumber, diced
- 1/2 cup of red onion, sliced
- 1/2 cup of kalamata olives, pitted
- 1/2 cup of grilled halloumi cheese, sliced
- 2 tablespoons of olive oil
- 1 tablespoon of red wine vinegar
- Salt and pepper to taste

Instructions:

1. Mix the mixed greens, cherry tomatoes, cucumber, red onion, and kalamata olives in a large bowl.
2. Warm 1 tablespoon of olive oil on medium heat in a separate pan.
3. Place the sliced halloumi cheese into the pan and cook for 2-3 minutes.
4. In a small bowl, combine 1 tablespoon of olive oil and 1 tablespoon of red wine vinegar, and whisk them together.
5. Next, pour the dressing over the mixed greens and vegetables and season with salt and pepper according to your taste.
6. Top the salad with the grilled halloumi cheese.

Nutrition Information (per serving):

Calories: 250 Fat: 20g Carbohydrates: 10g Protein: 12g Sodium: 500mg

MEDITERRANEAN BREAKFAST PITAS

Preparation time: 10 minutes

Cook time: 5 minutes

Servings: 2

Ingredients:

- 2 whole-grain pita pieces of bread
- 4 tablespoons hummus
- 4 ounces of smoked salmon
- 4 cherry tomatoes, sliced
- 1 avocado, sliced
- 4 tablespoons crumbled feta cheese
- 2 tablespoons chopped fresh dill
- Salt and pepper to taste

Instructions:

1. Heat a pan over medium heat.
2. Cut the pita bread in half to form pockets.
3. Toast the pita halves in the pan for 2-3 minutes on each side until slightly crispy.
4. Spread 2 tablespoons of hummus on the inside of each pita half.

5. Layer on the smoked salmon, cherry tomatoes, avocado slices, feta cheese, and dill.
6. Season with salt and pepper to taste.
7. Serve immediately and enjoy!

Nutrition Information (per serving):

Calories: 420 Fat: 22g Saturated Fat: 6g Cholesterol: 35mg Sodium: 960mg Carbohydrates: 44g Fiber: 11g Protein: 18g

MEDITERRANEAN BREAKFAST BOWL WITH GRILLED VEGETABLES AND POACHED EGG

Preparation time: 15 minutes

Cook time: 15 minutes

Servings: 1

Ingredients:

- 1 medium zucchini, sliced into rounds
- 1 medium red bell pepper, sliced into rounds
- 1 medium yellow onion, sliced into rounds
- 1 tablespoon olive oil
- Salt and pepper, to taste
- 1 large egg
- 1 slice whole grain bread
- 1 tablespoon crumbled feta cheese
- 1 tablespoon chopped fresh herbs (such as basil or parsley)

Instructions:

1. Heat a grill or grill pan to medium-high heat.
2. Mix the zucchini, red bell pepper, yellow onion, olive oil, salt, and pepper in a bowl. Toss to coat the vegetables evenly.
3. Grill the vegetables for about 8-10 minutes, occasionally flipping, until tender and slightly charred.
4. While the vegetables are grilled, bring a small pot of water to a boil. Lower the heat to a gentle simmer, then crack the egg into the water. Poach for 3-4 minutes until the white is set and the yolk is still runny.
5. Toast the slice of bread.
6. To assemble the breakfast bowl, arrange the grilled vegetables on the bottom, followed by the poached egg, the crumbled feta cheese, and the fresh herbs. Serve with the toasted bread on the side.

Nutrition Information (per serving):

Calories: 370 Fat: 23g Saturated Fat: 6g Cholesterol: 212mg Sodium: 755mg Carbohydrates: 29g Fiber: 7g Protein: 16g

MEDITERRANEAN STUFFED GRAPE LEAVES (DOLMADES)

Preparation time: 30 minutes
Cook time: 30 minutes
Servings: 4

Ingredients:

- 1 cup long-grain rice
- 1/2 cup chopped onion
- 1/4 cup chopped fresh parsley
- 2 tablespoons lemon juice
- 2 tablespoons olive oil
- 2 cloves garlic, minced
- 1/2 teaspoon dried mint
- Salt and black pepper, to taste
- 16-20 large grape leaves
- 1 lemon, sliced

Instructions:

1. One should heat 2 cups of water in a medium saucepan until it starts boiling. Stir in the rice, reduce the heat to low, and cook, covered, until tender and all the water has been absorbed about 18-20 minutes.
2. Combine the cooked rice, onion, parsley, lemon juice, olive oil, garlic, mint, salt, and pepper in a large bowl. Stir until well combined.
3. Rinse the grape leaves and pat dry. Place a heaping tablespoon of the rice mixture in the center of each leaf. Roll up the leaf tightly, tucking in the sides as you go, to form a neat package.
4. Arrange the stuffed grape leaves in a single layer in a large saucepan. Top with lemon slices. Add sufficient water to reach the halfway mark of the grape leaves sides.
5. Heat the water in a pot until it boils, then lower the heat and cover the pot. Let it simmer for around 30 minutes until the grape leaves become tender and the filling is heated.
6. If desired, serve the dolmades hot or at room temperature, garnished with additional lemon wedges.

Nutrition Information (per serving):

Calories: 200 Total Fat: 10 g Saturated Fat: 1.5 g Cholesterol: 0 mg Sodium: 130 mg Total Carbohydrates: 24 g Dietary Fiber: 2 g Protein: 4 g

MEDITERRANEAN ROASTED RED PEPPER HUMMUS

Preparation time: 10 minutes
Cook time: 10 minutes
Servings: 8

Ingredients:

- 1 can of chickpeas, drained and rinsed
- 2 medium-sized roasted red peppers
- 2 tablespoons of lemon juice
- 2 tablespoons of tahini
- 1 clove of garlic, minced
- 2 tablespoons of olive oil
- Salt and pepper, to taste

Instructions:

1. To start, set your oven to a temperature of 400°F (200°C).

2. Place the chickpeas and roasted red peppers on a baking sheet and roast for 10 minutes.
3. Please remove the roasted chickpeas and red peppers from the oven and allow them to cool down for a few minutes.
4. Combine chickpeas, red peppers, lemon juice, tahini, and minced garlic in a food processor.
5. Process until smooth, and then slowly add the olive oil while the food processor runs.
6. Season with salt and pepper to taste.
7. Serve the hummus with fresh vegetables, pita bread, or crackers.

Nutrition Information (per serving):
Calories: 170 Fat: 12g Saturated Fat: 2g Sodium: 160mg Carbohydrates: 12g Fiber: 3g Sugar: 2g Protein: 4g

MEDITERRANEAN STUFFED BELL PEPPERS

Preparation Time: 20 minutes

Cook Time: 30 minutes

Servings: 4

Ingredients:

- 4 large bell peppers, any color
- 1 lb ground turkey or chicken
- 1/2 cup diced onion
- 1/2 cup diced tomato
- 1/2 cup diced cucumber
- 1/4 cup chopped fresh parsley
- 1/4 cup chopped fresh mint
- 2 tbsp. olive oil
- 1 tsp. dried oregano
- 1 tsp. dried basil
- Salt and pepper, to taste
- 1/2 cup crumbled feta cheese

- 1/2 cup plain Greek yogurt

Instructions:
1. Preheat oven to 375°F (190°C).
2. Cut the stem from the bell peppers and remove the seeds and white membranes.
3. The onion should be added to a large skillet with olive oil and cooked over medium heat until it becomes soft and translucent, usually taking about 5 minutes.
4. Add the ground turkey or chicken to the skillet and cook until browned about 7-8 minutes.
5. Stir in the diced tomato, cucumber, parsley, mint, oregano, basil, salt, and pepper. Cook for another 2-3 minutes.
6. Stir in the crumbled feta cheese and remove the skillet from heat.
7. Spoon the mixture into the hollowed-out bell peppers and place them in a baking dish.
8. Bake the stuffed peppers in the oven for 20-25 minutes or until the peppers are cooked through, and the filling is heated.
9. Serve with a dollop of Greek yogurt on top. Enjoy!

Nutrition Information (per serving):
Calories: 347 Fat: 21g Saturated Fat: 7g Cholesterol: 98mg Sodium: 547mg Carbohydrates: 12g Fiber: 3g Sugar: 6g Protein: 27g

MEDITERRANEAN STUFFED MINI BELL PEPPERS

Preparation time: 10 minutes

Cook time: 20 minutes

Servings: 4

Ingredients:

- 8 mini bell peppers, sliced in half lengthwise and seeded
- 1 cup cooked quinoa
- 1 cup cherry tomatoes, diced
- 1/4 cup chopped kalamata olives
- 1/4 cup crumbled feta cheese
- 2 tablespoons chopped fresh basil
- 1 tablespoon olive oil
- Salt and pepper, to taste

Instructions:

1. The oven should be preheated to a temperature of 400°F (200°C).

2. Arrange the bell pepper halves, cut side up, on a baking sheet lined with parchment paper.
3. Combine the cooked quinoa, cherry tomatoes, olives, feta cheese, basil, and olive oil in a mixing bowl. Season with salt and pepper to taste.
4. Scoop the quinoa mixture using a spoon and distribute it evenly into each bell pepper half.
5. Bake in the oven for 20 minutes or until the bell peppers are tender and the filling is heated.
6. Serve warm as a snack or appetizer.

Nutrition Information (per serving):
Calories: 189 Fat: 11g Carbohydrates: 19g Fiber: 3g Protein: 7g

CRISPY BAKED ZUCCHINI FRITTERS

Preparation Time: 10 minutes
Cook Time: 20 minutes
Servings: 4

Ingredients:

- 2 medium zucchinis, grated
- 1/4 cup of all-purpose flour
- 1 egg, lightly beaten
- 1/4 cup of grated Parmesan cheese
- 2 tbsp of chopped fresh parsley
- 1 tsp of dried oregano
- Salt and pepper to taste
- Olive oil spray

Instructions:

1. Preheat oven to 400°F (200°C). Line a baking sheet with parchment paper.

2. Combine grated zucchini, flour, egg, Parmesan cheese, parsley, oregano, salt, and pepper in a large bowl. Mix well.
3. Place the mixture into small patties using a tablespoon on the prepared baking sheet.
4. Lightly spray the patties with olive oil spray.
5. Bake for 20 minutes or until golden brown and crispy.
6. Serve hot with a side of tzatziki sauce or hummus.

Nutrition Information (per serving):
Calories: 120 Fat: 8g Saturated Fat: 3g Cholesterol: 50mg Sodium: 350mg Carbohydrates: 9g Fiber: 2g Sugar: 3g Protein: 6g

GRILLED VEGETABLE PLATTER WITH HUMMUS AND PITA CHIPS

Preparation Time: 15 minutes
Cook Time: 20 minutes
Servings: 6

Ingredients:

- 1 large eggplant, sliced into 1/2-inch rounds
- 1 large zucchini, sliced into 1/2-inch rounds
- 1 large red bell pepper, sliced into 1/2-inch rounds
- 1 large yellow bell pepper, sliced into 1/2-inch rounds
- 2 tablespoons olive oil
- Salt and pepper, to taste
- 1 cup hummus
- 12 pita chips, store-bought or homemade

Instructions:

1. Preheat the grill to high heat.
2. Toss the eggplant, zucchini, red bell pepper, and yellow bell pepper with olive oil, salt, and pepper in a large bowl.

3. Grill the vegetables until tender and slightly charred, about 5-7 minutes on each side.
4. Serve the grilled vegetables on a large platter with the hummus and pita chips.

Nutrition Information (per serving):

Calories: 200 Fat: 12g Saturated Fat: 2g Cholesterol: 0mg Sodium: 380mg Carbohydrates: 20g
Fiber: 4g Sugar: 3g Protein: 6g

GRILLED EGGPLANT AND TOMATO SKEWERS

Preparation Time: 10 minutes

Cook Time: 10 minutes

Servings: 4

Ingredients:

- 2 medium eggplants, sliced into 1/2-inch rounds
- 2 medium tomatoes, sliced into 1/2-inch rounds
- 2 tablespoons olive oil
- 1 teaspoon dried basil
- 1 teaspoon dried oregano
- Salt and pepper, to taste
- 2 tablespoons balsamic vinegar
- 2 tablespoons chopped fresh parsley

Instructions:

1. Preheat the grill to medium-high heat.
2. Mix olive oil, basil, oregano, salt, and pepper in a small bowl.
3. Alternately thread eggplant and tomato slices onto four skewers.

4. Brush the skewers with the olive oil mixture.
5. Grill the skewers for 5 minutes on each side until the vegetables are tender and lightly charred.
6. Drizzle balsamic vinegar over the skewers and sprinkle with chopped parsley.
7. Serve hot or at room temperature as an appetizer or snack.

Nutrition Information (per serving):
Calories: 127 Fat: 9.9 g Saturated Fat: 1.3 g Carbohydrates: 11.4 g Fiber: 4.8 g Protein: 2.6 g

SPICED CHICKPEA AND CUCUMBER BITES

Preparation Time: 10 minutes

Cook Time: 0 minutes

Servings: 4

Ingredients:

- 1 can chickpeas, drained and rinsed
- 1 large cucumber, sliced into rounds
- 1/4 cup plain Greek yogurt
- 1 teaspoon ground cumin
- 1 teaspoon paprika
- 1/2 teaspoon garlic powder
- 1/4 teaspoon salt
- 1/4 teaspoon black pepper
- 1 tablespoon lemon juice
- Fresh parsley or cilantro for garnish

Instructions:

1. In a bowl, mash the chickpeas with a fork until they are broken down into small pieces.
2. Stir in the Greek yogurt, cumin, paprika, garlic powder, salt, pepper, and lemon juice until well combined.
3. Spoon the chickpea mixture onto each cucumber slice and top with fresh parsley or cilantro.
4. Serve immediately or chill in the refrigerator until ready to serve.

Nutrition Information (per serving):

Calories: 140 Fat: 4g Carbohydrates: 19g Protein: 8g Fiber: 5g Sugar: 4g

MEDITERRANEAN GRILLED ZUCCHINI ROLL-UPS WITH HERBED CREAM CHEESE

Preparation time: 15 minutes

Cook time: 10 minutes

Servings: 4

Ingredients:

- 2 medium zucchinis, sliced lengthwise into 1/4 inch thick slices
- 4 oz. cream cheese, softened
- 2 tbsp. chopped fresh herbs (such as basil, parsley, and chives)
- Salt and pepper, to taste
- 4 thin slices of deli ham or prosciutto
- 4 tbsp. sun-dried tomatoes, drained and chopped

Instructions:

1. Preheat your grill to medium heat.
2. Mix the cream cheese, herbs, salt, and pepper in a medium bowl until well combined.
3. Spread a thin layer of the cream cheese mixture on each zucchini slice.

4. Place a slice of ham or prosciutto on the cream cheese mixture, followed by a sprinkle of sun-dried tomatoes.
5. Roll up each slice of zucchini and secure it with a toothpick.
6. Place the zucchini roll-ups on the grill and cook on each side for 5-7 minutes until they are slightly charred and tender.
7. Serve hot as an appetizer or snack.

Nutrition Information (per serving):
Calories: 150 Fat: 12 g Carbohydrates: 7 g Protein: 5 g Fiber: 2 g

GRILLED EGGPLANT AND FETA BITES

Preparation time: 10 minutes
Cook time: 10 minutes
Servings: 4

Ingredients:

- 1 medium eggplant, sliced into 1/2-inch rounds
- 1/2 cup crumbled feta cheese
- 2 tablespoons chopped fresh basil
- 2 tablespoons extra-virgin olive oil
- Salt and pepper to taste
- Lemon wedges for serving

Instructions:

1. Preheat a grill or grill pan over medium heat.
2. In a small bowl, mix the feta cheese and basil.
3. Here's a possible paraphrase: Coat the eggplant slices with olive oil on both sides and sprinkle them with salt and pepper.

4. Grill the eggplant slices on each side for about 4-5 minutes or until tender and lightly charred.
5. Once the eggplant slices are grilled to your liking, take them off the heat and add a dollop of the feta cheese mixture on top of each slice.
6. Serve the eggplant bites with lemon wedges on the side.

Nutrition Information (per serving):

Calories: 140 Fat: 12g Saturated Fat: 4g Cholesterol: 20mg Sodium: 300mg Carbohydrates: 7g Fiber: 3g Protein: 5g

SOUPS AND SALADS

MEDITERRANEAN CHICKPEA AND VEGETABLE SALAD

Preparation Time: 10 minutes
Cook Time: 10 minutes
Servings: 4

Ingredients:

- 1 can of chickpeas, drained and rinsed
- 1 red bell pepper, chopped
- 1 yellow bell pepper, chopped
- 1 large cucumber, chopped
- 1 cup cherry tomatoes, halved
- 1/2 red onion, sliced
- 1/4 cup pitted Kalamata olives
- 1/4 cup crumbled feta cheese
- 2 tablespoons extra-virgin olive oil

- 1 tablespoon lemon juice
- 1 garlic clove, minced
- Salt and pepper, to taste

Instructions:
1. Combine chickpeas, red and yellow bell peppers, cucumber, cherry tomatoes, red onion, and Kalamata olives in a large bowl.
2. Whisk together olive oil, lemon juice, garlic, salt, and pepper in a small bowl.
3. Pour the dressing over the vegetable mixture and gently toss to combine.
4. Sprinkle with crumbled feta cheese.
5. Serve immediately or refrigerate for later.

Nutrition Information (per serving):
Calories: 250 Total Fat: 18g Saturated Fat: 5g Cholesterol: 15mg Sodium: 460mg Total Carbohydrates: 20g Dietary Fiber: 5g Sugars: 7g Protein: 7g

MEDITERRANEAN CHICKPEA SALAD

Preparation Time: 15 minutes
Cook Time: N/A
Servings: 4

Ingredients:

- 2 cans of chickpeas, drained and rinsed
- 1 large red bell pepper, diced
- 1 large yellow bell pepper, diced
- 1 large cucumber, peeled and diced
- 1 large red onion, diced
- 1/2 cup of cherry tomatoes, halved
- 1/4 cup of kalamata olives, pitted and halved
- 1/4 cup of crumbled feta cheese
- 2 tbsp of freshly squeezed lemon juice
- 2 tbsp of extra-virgin olive oil

- 1 tsp of dried oregano
- Salt and pepper, to taste

Instructions:

1. Combine chickpeas, red bell pepper, yellow bell pepper, cucumber, red onion, cherry tomatoes, and kalamata olives in a large mixing bowl.
2. Whisk together the lemon juice, extra-virgin olive oil, oregano, salt, and pepper in a small mixing bowl.
3. Pour the dressing over the chickpea mixture and toss until everything is evenly coated.
4. Gently fold in the feta cheese.
5. Serve the Mediterranean Chickpea Salad as a side dish, or enjoy it as a light and healthy meal.

Nutrition Information (per serving):

Calories: 250 Fat: 14g Saturated Fat: 4g Cholesterol: 15mg Sodium: 460mg Carbohydrates: 26g Fiber: 7g Sugar: 6g Protein: 9g

TOMATO AND CUCUMBER SALAD

Preparation time: 15 minutes

Cook time: 0 minutes

Servings: 4

Ingredients:

- 4 medium-sized ripe tomatoes, chopped
- 2 medium-sized cucumbers, peeled and chopped
- 1 red onion, thinly sliced
- 1/4 cup of fresh basil leaves, chopped
- 3 tablespoons of extra-virgin olive oil
- 2 tablespoons of red wine vinegar
- Salt and pepper to taste

Instructions:

1. Combine the chopped tomatoes, cucumbers, red onion, and basil in a large bowl.
2. Whisk the extra-virgin olive oil, red wine vinegar, salt, and pepper in a small bowl.
3. Pour the dressing over the tomato and cucumber mixture and gently toss to combine.

4. Serve the salad immediately, or refrigerate until ready to serve.

Nutrition Information (per serving):
Calories: 162 Fat: 15.6 g Saturated Fat: 2.1 g Cholesterol: 0 mg Sodium: 73 mg Carbohydrates: 9.4 g Fiber: 2.5 g Sugar: 5.5 g Protein: 1.7 g

LEMON AND CHICKPEA SOUP

Preparation time: 10 minutes
Cook time: 25 minutes
Servings: 4

Ingredients:

- 1 tablespoon olive oil
- 1 onion, chopped
- 2 cloves garlic, minced
- 2 cans chickpeas, drained and rinsed
- 4 cups vegetable broth
- 1 teaspoon dried thyme
- 1/2 teaspoon salt
- 1/4 teaspoon black pepper
- 3 tablespoons lemon juice

- 2 tablespoons chopped fresh parsley

Instructions:
1. Heat the olive oil in a large pot over medium heat.
2. Add the onion and garlic and cook until softened about 5 minutes.
3. Add the chickpeas, broth, thyme, salt, and pepper to the pot.
4. Bring to a boil, then reduce heat and simmer for 20 minutes.
5. Using an immersion blender, puree the soup until smooth.
6. Stir in the lemon juice and parsley.
7. Serve hot.

Nutrition Information (per serving):
Calories: 191 Fat: 7g Carbohydrates: 26g Protein: 9g Fiber: 7g Sodium: 844mg

GRILLED EGGPLANT AND BELL PEPPER SALAD

Preparation Time: 20 minutes

Cook Time: 15 minutes

Servings: 4

Ingredients:

- 2 medium eggplants, sliced into rounds
- 2 large red bell peppers, sliced into rounds
- 2 tablespoons olive oil
- Salt and black pepper, to taste
- 1 clove garlic, minced
- 3 tablespoons red wine vinegar
- 1 teaspoon dried oregano
- 1 teaspoon dried basil
- 1/4 cup crumbled feta cheese

Instructions:

1. Preheat the grill to medium-high heat.
2. Brush the eggplant and bell pepper rounds with olive oil and season with salt and black pepper.
3. Place the eggplant and bell peppers on the grill and cook for 7-8 minutes on each side until slightly charred and tender.
4. Remove from the grill and let cool.
5. Whisk together the garlic, red wine vinegar, oregano, basil, and olive oil in a small bowl. Season with salt and black pepper.
6. In a large bowl, place the grilled eggplant and bell peppers.
7. Pour the dressing over the vegetables and toss to combine.
8. Sprinkle the crumbled feta cheese on top.
9. Enjoy the dish immediately, or if you prefer, you can refrigerate it until you're ready to serve it.

Nutrition Information (per serving):

Calories: 200 Fat: 16g Saturated Fat: 3g Carbohydrates: 12g Fiber: 6g Protein: 5g Sodium: 300mg

TOMATO AND CUCUMBER SALAD WITH FETA

Preparation Time: 15 minutes
Cook Time: 0 minutes
Servings: 4

Ingredients:

- 2 large ripe tomatoes, diced
- 1 large cucumber, peeled and diced
- 1/4 cup diced red onion
- 1/4 cup crumbled feta cheese
- 2 tablespoons extra-virgin olive oil
- 2 tablespoons freshly squeezed lemon juice
- 1 garlic clove, minced
- Season with salt and freshly ground black pepper according to your taste.
- Fresh parsley or basil leaves for garnish (optional)

Instructions:

1. Combine the diced tomatoes, cucumber, red onion, and feta cheese in a large bowl.

2. Whisk the olive oil, lemon juice, and minced garlic in a small bowl. Season with salt and pepper to taste.
3. Pour the dressing over the tomato and cucumber mixture and toss to combine.
4. Serve the salad immediately, garnished with parsley or basil leaves if desired.

Nutrition Information (per serving):
Calories: 170 Fat: 15 g Saturated Fat: 4 g Cholesterol: 20 mg Sodium: 220 mg Carbohydrates: 9 g Fiber: 2 g Sugar: 4 g Protein: 4 g

TOMATO AND CUCUMBER SALAD WITH WHITE BEAN SOUP

Preparation time: 15 minutes
Cook time: 20 minutes
Servings: 4

Ingredients:
<u>For the salad:</u>

- 2 large tomatoes, chopped
- 1 large cucumber, chopped
- 1/4 red onion, finely chopped
- 2 tbsp olive oil
- 1 tbsp red wine vinegar
- 1 tsp dried oregano
- Salt and pepper, to taste

For the soup:

- 1 tbsp olive oil
- 1 large onion, chopped
- 3 garlic cloves, minced
- Two cans of white beans, weighing 15 ounces, have been drained and rinsed.
- 4 cups chicken or vegetable broth
- 1 tsp dried thyme
- Salt and pepper, to taste

Instructions:

1. For the salad: In a large bowl, combine the chopped tomatoes, cucumber, and red onion.
2. Combine olive oil, red wine vinegar, oregano, salt, and pepper in a small bowl and whisk them together.
3. Pour the dressing over the tomato and cucumber mixture, tossing to coat evenly.
4. Heat the olive oil over medium heat in a large saucepan for the soup.
5. Add the onion and garlic and cook until softened about 5 minutes.
6. Add the white beans, broth, thyme, salt, and pepper.
7. Bring the mixture to a boil, then reduce heat and simmer for 15 minutes.
8. Use an immersion or regular blender to blend the soup until it reaches a smooth consistency.
9. Serve hot soup, topped with tomato and cucumber salad on the side.

Nutrition Information (per serving):

Calories: 300 Fat: 12g Carbohydrates: 36g Protein: 12g Fiber: 8g Sodium: 800mg

MEDITERRANEAN CHICKPEA AND TOMATO SALAD

Preparation Time: 10 minutes

Cook Time: 0 minutes

Servings: 4

Ingredients:

- 2 cans of chickpeas, drained and rinsed
- 2 large tomatoes, chopped
- 1/2 red onion, thinly sliced
- 1/4 cup kalamata olives, pitted
- 1/4 cup crumbled feta cheese
- 2 tbsp. lemon juice
- 2 tbsp. extra-virgin olive oil
- 1 tsp. dried oregano
- Salt and pepper, to taste

Instructions:

1. In a large bowl, combine chickpeas, tomatoes, red onion, olives, and feta cheese.
2. Whisk together the lemon juice, olive oil, oregano, salt, and pepper in a small bowl.
3. Pour the dressing over the salad and mix well.
4. Serve chilled or at room temperature.

Nutrition Information (per serving):

Calories: 220 Fat: 12g Saturated Fat: 3g Cholesterol: 10mg Sodium: 480mg Carbohydrates: 21g Fiber: 6g Sugar: 4g Protein: 9g

TOMATO AND CUCUMBER SALAD RECI

Preparation Time: 10 minutes
Cook Time: N/A
Servings: 4

Ingredients:
- 4 medium tomatoes, diced
- 2 medium cucumbers, peeled and diced
- 1 red onion, thinly sliced
- 1/4 cup pitted Kalamata olives
- 2 tablespoons red wine vinegar ∙ ∩ ᴓ
- 3 tablespoons olive oil
- Salt and pepper, to taste
- 2 tablespoons freshly chopped basil

Instructions:
1. Combine diced tomatoes, cucumbers, red onion, and Kalamata olives in a large bowl.
2. Whisk together red wine vinegar, olive oil, salt, and pepper in a small bowl.
3. Pour the dressing over the tomato and cucumber mixture and toss to combine.
4. Let the salad sit for 5-10 minutes to allow the flavors to meld.

5. Before serving, sprinkle with freshly chopped basil.

Nutrition Information (per serving):

Calories: 165 Total Fat: 15 g Saturated Fat: 2 g Sodium: 243 mg Total Carbohydrates: 9 g Dietary Fiber: 2 g Sugars: 5 g Protein: 2 g

LENTIL AND KALE SALAD WITH LEMON VINAIGRETTE

Preparation Time: 15 minutes
Cook Time: 15 minutes
Servings: 4

Ingredients:

- 1 cup brown lentils
- 4 cups water
- 2 bunches kale, stems removed and chopped
- 1 cup cherry tomatoes, halved
- 1/2 red onion, thinly sliced
- 1/2 cup crumbled feta cheese
- 1/4 cup freshly squeezed lemon juice
- 2 tablespoons olive oil
- 1 clove garlic, minced
- Salt and pepper, to taste

Instructions:

1. Rinse the lentils and add them to a pot with water. Bring the water to a boil, lower the heat, and let it simmer for about 15 minutes until the lentils become tender. Drain the water and keep the lentils aside.
2. Combine the cooked lentils, kale, cherry tomatoes, red onion, and feta cheese in a large bowl.
3. Whisk together the lemon juice, olive oil, garlic, salt, and pepper in a small bowl to make the vinaigrette.
4. Drizzle the vinaigrette over the salad and toss gently to coat. You can serve the salad immediately or refrigerate it until ready to serve.

Nutrition Information (per serving):

Calories: 297 Fat: 13g Carbohydrates: 35g Fiber: 14g Protein: 14g

MEDITERRANEAN LENTIL SOUP

Preparation Time: 10 minutes
Cook Time: 30 minutes
Servings: 4

Ingredients:
- 1 tbsp olive oil
- 1 onion, chopped
- 2 garlic cloves, minced
- 2 carrots, chopped
- 2 celery stalks, chopped
- 1 cup green lentils
- 4 cups vegetable broth
- 1 can of diced tomatoes (14 oz)
- 1 tsp dried oregano
- 1 tsp dried thyme
- Salt and pepper to taste

- 2 tbsp chopped fresh parsley

Instructions:
1. In a large saucepan, heat the olive oil over medium heat.
2. Add the onion, garlic, carrots, celery, and sauté for 5-7 minutes until the vegetables are softened.
3. Stir in the green lentils, vegetable broth, diced tomatoes, oregano, thyme, salt, and pepper.
4. Bring the mixture to a boil, then reduce heat and let it simmer for 20-25 minutes or until the lentils are tender.
5. Serve hot, garnished with fresh parsley.

Nutrition Information (per serving):
Calories: 200 Fat: 5g Saturated Fat: 1g Cholesterol: 0mg Sodium: 800mg Carbohydrates: 30g Fiber: 8g Sugar: 6g Protein: 10g

MEDITERRANEAN FISH SOUP RECIPE

Preparation time: 15 minutes
Cook time: 25 minutes
Servings: 4

Ingredients:

- 1 large onion, chopped
- 2 large garlic cloves, minced
- 2 medium tomatoes, chopped
- 2 medium carrots, chopped
- 2 medium potatoes, peeled and chopped
- 1 cup chopped fennel bulb
- 4 cups fish stock or chicken broth
- 1 cup white wine
- 1 tsp. dried thyme
- Salt and pepper, to taste

- 1/4 tsp. saffron threads
- 1 lb. firm white fish fillets, such as cod or haddock, cut into 2-inch pieces
- 1 cup cooked white beans, such as cannellini or navy beans
- 2 tbsp. lemon juice
- 2 tbsp. Chopped fresh parsley

Instructions:

1. Heat 2 tablespoons of olive oil over medium heat in a large saucepan or Dutch oven.
2. Add the onion and garlic and cook until softened about 5 minutes.
3. Add the tomatoes, carrots, potatoes, fennel, stock or broth, wine, thyme, salt, pepper, and saffron. Bring to a boil, then reduce heat and simmer for 15 minutes.
4. Stir in the fish and beans and cook until the fish is cooked about 5 minutes.
5. Stir in the lemon juice and parsley, and serve hot.

Nutrition Information (per serving):

Calories: 300 Fat: 7 g Saturated Fat: 1 g Cholesterol: 70 mg Sodium: 730 mg Carbohydrates: 25 g Fiber: 7 g Sugar: 7 g Protein: 28 g

MEDITERRANEAN SALMON SOUP

Preparation Time: 15 minutes

Cook Time: 20 minutes

Servings: 4

Ingredients:
- 1 lb salmon fillets, skinless
- 2 tbsp olive oil
- 1 medium onion, diced
- 2 cloves garlic, minced
- 2 medium carrots, diced
- 2 celery stalks, diced
- 2 tbsp tomato paste
- 4 cups chicken or vegetable broth
- 1 can (15 oz) chickpeas, drained and rinsed
- 1 cup frozen peas
- 1 tsp dried oregano
- Salt and pepper, to taste

- Fresh parsley, chopped, for garnish

Instructions:
1. Heat the olive oil in a large pot over medium heat.
2. Add the onion and cook until soft, about 5 minutes.
3. Add the garlic, carrots, and celery and cook for another 5 minutes.
4. Stir in the tomato paste and cook for 2 minutes.
5. Pour in the broth, chickpeas, frozen peas, and oregano. Season with salt and pepper.
6. Bring the soup to a simmer and cook for 10 minutes.
7. Add the salmon fillets to the soup until they are cooked through, about 5 minutes.
8. Serve the soup hot, garnished with fresh parsley.

Nutrition Information (per serving):
Calories: 365 Fat: 20g Carbohydrates: 20g Protein: 28g Sodium: 822mg Fiber: 6g

MEDITERRANEAN SALMON AND FETA SOUP

Preparation time: 10 minutes
Cook time: 20 minutes
Servings: 4

Ingredients:

- 2 tablespoons olive oil
- 1 onion, chopped
- 2 cloves garlic, minced
- 4 cups chicken broth
- 1 cup chopped tomato
- 1 cup chopped carrots
- 1 cup chopped celery
- 1 teaspoon dried basil
- 1 teaspoon dried oregano
- Salt and pepper, to taste
- 1 pound salmon fillet, skinned and cut into 1-inch pieces
- 1/2 cup crumbled feta cheese
- 2 tablespoons chopped fresh parsley

Instructions:

1. Heat the olive oil in a large pot over medium heat. Add the chopped onion and minced garlic, and cook until they become soft, which takes around 3 minutes.
2. Add the chicken broth, tomato, carrots, celery, basil, oregano, salt, and pepper to the pot and boil.
3. Reduce heat and simmer for 10 minutes until the vegetables are tender.
4. Add the salmon pieces to the soup and cook for another 5 minutes until the salmon is cooked.
5. Stir in the feta cheese and parsley. Serve hot.

Nutrition Information (per serving):

Calories: 333 Fat: 21 g Saturated Fat: 6 g Cholesterol: 63 mg Sodium: 865 mg Carbohydrates: 15 g Fiber: 3 g Protein: 24 g

MEDITERRANEAN CHICKEN AND RICE SOUP

Preparation time: 10 minutes

Cook time: 25 minutes

Servings: 4

Ingredients:

- 1 tablespoon olive oil
- 1 large onion, chopped
- 2 cloves garlic, minced
- 1 teaspoon dried thyme
- 1 teaspoon dried oregano
- 1/2 teaspoon paprika
- 1/4 teaspoon cumin
- 1/4 teaspoon red pepper flakes (optional)
- 1 cup long-grain white rice
- 4 cups chicken broth
- 2 cups water
- 1 large carrot, diced
- 1 large stalk of celery, diced

- 1 cup chopped cooked chicken
- 1 can (14.5 ounces) diced tomatoes
- Salt and pepper, to taste
- 1/4 cup chopped fresh parsley
- 1/4 cup crumbled feta cheese (optional)

Instructions:

1. In a large pot, heat the olive oil over medium heat.
2. Add the onion and cook until soft, about 5 minutes.
3. Add the garlic, thyme, oregano, paprika, cumin, and red pepper flakes (if using) and cook for 1 minute.
4. Stir in the rice and cook for 2 minutes.
5. Add the chicken broth, water, carrot, celery, chicken, and diced tomatoes.
6. Bring to a boil, then reduce heat and simmer for 20 minutes or until the rice is tender.
7. Season with salt and pepper to taste.
8. Stir in the parsley and feta cheese (if using) and serve.

Nutrition Information (per serving):

Calories: 220 Fat: 7 g Saturated Fat: 2 g Cholesterol: 40 mg Sodium: 480 mg Carbohydrates: 26 g Fiber: 2 g Sugar: 3 g Protein: 14 g

MEDITERRANEAN GARBANZO SOUP RECIPE

Preparation Time: 15 minutes
Cook Time: 35 minutes
Servings: 4

Ingredients:

- 2 tablespoons of olive oil
- 1 large onion, chopped
- 3 cloves of garlic, minced
- 1 large carrot, diced
- 1 large celery stalk, diced
- 2 cans of garbanzo beans, drained and rinsed
- 4 cups of vegetable broth
- 1 large tomato, chopped
- 1 teaspoon of dried thyme
- 1 teaspoon of dried basil
- 1/2 teaspoon of salt
- 1/4 teaspoon of black pepper
- 1 cup of fresh spinach leaves, chopped

- 1/2 cup of crumbled feta cheese

Instructions:

1. In a large pot, heat the olive oil over medium heat.
2. Add the chopped onion and minced garlic and cook until the onion is translucent about 5 minutes.
3. Stir in the diced carrot and celery and cook for another 5 minutes.
4. Add the garbanzo beans, vegetable broth, chopped tomato, thyme, basil, salt, and pepper.
5. Increase the heat to high and bring the soup to a boil.
6. Reduce the heat to medium-low and let the soup simmer for 20 minutes.
7. Stir in the chopped spinach and let the soup cook for 5 minutes.
8. Serve the soup hot, topped with crumbled feta cheese.

Nutrition Information (per serving):

Calories: 304 Fat: 15g Protein: 12g Carbohydrates: 36g Fiber: 9g Sodium: 947mg

THREE BEAN MEDITERRANEAN SOUP RECIPE

Preparation time: 15 minutes

Cook time: 45 minutes

Servings: 6

Ingredients:

- 1 tablespoon olive oil
- 1 onion, diced
- 3 garlic cloves, minced
- 1 red bell pepper, diced
- 1 teaspoon ground cumin
- 1 teaspoon dried oregano
- 1/2 teaspoon red pepper flakes
- 4 cups vegetable broth
- 1 can (15 ounces) chickpeas, drained and rinsed
- 1 can (15 ounces) of kidney beans, drained and rinsed
- 1 can (15 ounces) of white beans, drained and rinsed
- 1 can (14.5 ounces) diced tomatoes
- 1/2 teaspoon salt

- 1/4 teaspoon black pepper
- 1/4 cup chopped fresh parsley
- 1/4 cup chopped fresh cilantro

Instructions:

1. Heat the oil in a large pot over medium heat.
2. Add the onion, garlic, and red bell pepper and cook for 5 minutes or until the vegetables are soft.
3. Stir in the cumin, oregano, and red pepper flakes and cook for 1 minute.
4. Add the pot's broth, chickpeas, kidney beans, white beans, tomatoes, salt, and black pepper.
5. Bring the soup to a boil, then reduce heat to low and let it simmer for 30 minutes.
6. Stir in the parsley and cilantro just before serving.

Nutrition Information (per serving):

Calories: 223 Fat: 5 g Saturated Fat: 1 g Cholesterol: 0 mg Sodium: 611 mg Carbohydrates: 36 g Fiber: 9 g Sugar: 7 g Protein: 12 g

MEDITERRANEAN-STYLE SEAFOOD SOUP RECIPE

Preparation time: 10 minutes

Cook time: 20 minutes

Servings: 4

Ingredients:

- 1 tablespoon olive oil
- 1 onion, chopped
- 3 cloves garlic, minced
- 2 carrots, peeled and chopped
- 2 celery stalks, chopped
- 1 fennel bulb, chopped
- 1 teaspoon dried thyme
- 1 teaspoon dried basil
- 1 can (28 ounces) diced tomatoes
- 4 cups chicken or seafood stock

- 1 cup white wine
- 1 cup chopped fish fillets (such as cod or halibut)
- 1 cup chopped raw shrimp
- 1 cup chopped clams
- Salt and pepper to taste
- 1 cup cooked white beans
- 2 tablespoons chopped fresh parsley

Instructions:

1. Heat the olive oil in a large pot over medium heat. Add the onion, garlic, carrots, celery, and fennel, and cook for about 5 minutes until the vegetables are tender.
2. Stir in the thyme, basil, diced tomatoes, chicken or seafood stock, and white wine. Bring the soup to a boil, then reduce the heat to low and let it simmer for about 10 minutes.
3. Add the fish fillets, shrimp, and clams to the pot and cook for about 5 minutes or until the seafood is cooked.
4. Season the soup with salt and pepper to taste. Stir in the cooked white beans and parsley.
5. Serve the soup hot with crusty bread.

Nutrition Information (per serving):

Calories: 220 Total Fat: 6g Saturated Fat: 1g Cholesterol: 75mg Sodium: 570mg Total Carbohydrates: 17g Dietary Fiber: 4g Protein: 23g

MEDITERRANEAN WHITE BEAN SOUP

Preparation time: 15 minutes

Cook time: 45 minutes

Servings: 4

Ingredients:

- 1 tablespoon olive oil
- 1 medium onion, diced
- 2 cloves of garlic, minced
- 2 carrots, peeled and diced
- 2 celery stalks, diced
- 1 teaspoon dried thyme
- 1 teaspoon dried basil
- 1/2 teaspoon dried oregano
- 1 can (14.5 oz) diced tomatoes
- 4 cups vegetable broth
- 2 cans (15 oz each) of cannellini beans, drained and rinsed

- 1 cup chopped kale
- Salt and pepper, to taste
- 1 lemon, juiced
- Fresh parsley, chopped, for garnish

Instructions:
1. In a large saucepan, heat the olive oil over medium heat.
2. Add the onion, garlic, carrots, and celery, and cook until the vegetables are soft and translucent about 5 minutes.
3. Stir in the thyme, basil, and oregano, and cook for 1 minute.
4. Add the diced tomatoes, vegetable broth, cannellini beans, and kale to the saucepan.
5. After bringing the soup to a boil, lower the heat and let it simmer for 30 minutes
6. Season the soup with salt and pepper to taste.
7. Stir in the lemon juice just before serving.
8. Serve the soup hot, garnished with fresh parsley.

Nutrition Information (per serving):
Calories: 250 Fat: 5g Saturated Fat: 1g Cholesterol: 0mg Sodium: 740mg Carbohydrates: 43g Fiber: 9g Sugar: 8g Protein: 12g

MEDITERRANEAN GRILLED CHICKEN WITH OLIVE TAPENADE

Preparation time: 20 minutes

Cook time: 20 minutes

Servings: 4

Ingredients:

- 4 boneless, skinless chicken breasts
- 1/2 cup kalamata olives, pitted
- 1/4 cup chopped fresh parsley
- 3 cloves garlic, minced
- 2 tablespoons capers, drained
- 2 tablespoons lemon juice
- 1/4 cup extra-virgin olive oil
- Salt and pepper to taste

Instructions:

1. Preheat the grill to medium-high heat.

2. Combine the olives, parsley, garlic, capers, lemon juice, and olive oil in a food processor. Blend until the mixture forms a coarse paste.
3. Season the chicken breasts with salt and pepper and brush both sides with the olive tapenade.
4. Place the chicken on the grill and cook for 5 to 7 minutes per side until the internal temperature reaches 165°F.
5. Serve the chicken with additional olive tapenade on the side.

Nutrition Information (per serving):
Calories: 394 Fat: 28g Saturated Fat: 4g Cholesterol: 93mg Sodium: 684mg Carbohydrates: 4g Fiber: 2g Protein: 35g

MEDITERRANEAN GRILLED CHICKEN WITH TOMATO, CUCUMBER, AND FETA SALAD

Preparation time: 15 minutes
Cook time: 20 minutes
Servings: 4

Ingredients:
- 4 boneless, skinless chicken breasts
- 1/4 cup olive oil
- 2 cloves garlic, minced
- 1 teaspoon dried oregano
- 1/2 teaspoon salt
- 1/4 teaspoon black pepper
- 2 medium tomatoes, diced
- 1 medium cucumber, peeled and diced
- 1/4 cup crumbled feta cheese
- 2 tablespoons lemon juice
- 1 tablespoon red wine vinegar
- 2 tablespoons chopped fresh parsley

Instructions:

1. Preheat the grill to medium heat.
2. Whisk the olive oil, garlic, oregano, salt, and pepper in a small bowl.
3. Place the chicken breasts in a large shallow dish and pour the marinade over the top. Let marinate for 10 minutes.
4. Meanwhile, in a large bowl, combine the tomatoes, cucumber, feta cheese, lemon juice, red wine vinegar, and parsley. Toss to combine.
5. Place the chicken on the grill and cook for about 10 minutes on each side until fully cooked.
6. Serve the chicken with the tomato, cucumber, and feta salad on the side.

Nutrition Information (per serving):

Calories: 350 Fat: 23g Saturated Fat: 6g Cholesterol: 94mg Sodium: 590mg Carbohydrates: 8g Fiber: 2g Sugar: 3g Protein: 33g

MEDITERRANEAN WHITE BEAN SOUP WITH KALE AND SAUSAGE

Preparation Time: 15 minutes

Cook Time: 45 minutes

Servings: 4

Ingredients:

- 1 tablespoon olive oil
- 1 large onion, chopped
- 3 garlic cloves, minced
- 4 ounces of Italian sausage, casings removed
- 2 cans (15 ounces each) of white beans, drained and rinsed
- 4 cups of chicken broth
- 1 teaspoon dried thyme
- 1/2 teaspoon dried basil
- 1/4 teaspoon red pepper flakes
- Salt and pepper, to taste

- 4 cups of kale, chopped
- 1/4 cup of grated Parmesan cheese
- Freshly squeezed lemon juice for serving

Instructions:
1. In a large pot, heat the olive oil over medium heat. Add the onion and cook until soft, about 5 minutes.
2. Add the garlic and sausage to the pot and cook until browned about 5 minutes.
3. Add the white beans, chicken broth, thyme, basil, red pepper flakes, salt, and pepper to the pot. Bring the soup to a boil and then reduce heat to a simmer.
4. Cook the soup for 25-30 minutes until the flavors have melded together.
5. Stir in the chopped kale and continue to cook until the kale is wilted about 5 minutes.
6. Garnish the soup with grated Parmesan cheese and a squeeze of lemon juice before serving.

Nutrition Information (per serving):
Calories: 391 Fat: 20g Saturated Fat: 6g Cholesterol: 43mg Sodium: 1254mg Carbohydrates: 36g Fiber: 11g Protein: 20g

MAIN DISH
RECIPES

MEDITERRANEAN BAKED CHICKEN WITH TOMATOES AND OLIVES

Preparation Time: 10 minutes
Cook Time: 45 minutes
Servings: 4

Ingredients:

- 4 boneless, skinless chicken breasts
- 1 cup cherry tomatoes, halved
- 1/2 cup kalamata olives, pitted and halved
- 1/4 cup chopped fresh parsley
- 4 cloves garlic, minced
- 1/4 cup extra-virgin olive oil
- Salt and pepper to taste
- 1 lemon, sliced into rounds

Instructions:

1. Preheat oven to 375°F (190°C).
2. In a large mixing bowl, combine cherry tomatoes, olives, parsley, garlic, olive oil, salt, and pepper. Mix well.

3. Arrange chicken breasts in a single layer in a large baking dish.
4. Spoon the tomato mixture over the chicken breasts, distributing it evenly.
5. Place lemon slices over the tomato mixture.
6. Bake for 40-45 minutes until the chicken is cooked and the tomatoes tender and slightly caramelized.
7. Serve hot with crusty bread or over a bed of cooked quinoa or rice.

Nutrition Information (per serving):
Calories: 480 Fat: 32g Carbohydrates: 11g Protein: 39g Sodium: 730mg

MEDITERRANEAN GRILLED CHICKEN WITH CAULIFLOWER RICE AND ROASTED VEGETABLES

Preparation time: 15 minutes

Cook time: 30 minutes

Servings: 4

Ingredients:

- 4 boneless, skinless chicken breasts
- 1 tsp. dried basil
- 1 tsp. dried oregano
- 1 tsp. dried thyme
- 1 tsp. garlic powder
- Salt and pepper, to taste
- 1 tbsp. olive oil
- 1 head of cauliflower, chopped into florets
- 1 red bell pepper, chopped
- 1 yellow bell pepper, chopped

- 1 zucchini, chopped
- 1 yellow squash, chopped
- 2 tbsp. balsamic vinegar

Instructions:

1. Preheat your grill to medium-high heat.
2. Mix basil, oregano, thyme, garlic powder, salt, and pepper in a small bowl. Rub this mixture onto both sides of the chicken breasts.
3. Mix the chopped red and yellow bell peppers, zucchini, and squash in a large bowl. Drizzle with 1 tablespoon of olive oil and season with salt and pepper.
4. Place the chicken breasts and the mixed vegetables on the grill. Grill the chicken for 6-8 minutes per side or until its internal temperature reaches 165°F.
5. While the chicken and vegetables are cooking, prepare the cauliflower rice. First, chop the cauliflower into florets and place it in a food processor. Pulse until the cauliflower resembles rice.
6. Heat 1 tablespoon of olive oil over medium heat in a large pan. Add the cauliflower rice and cook for 5-7 minutes, occasionally stirring, until tender.
7. Serve the grilled chicken on top of the cauliflower rice and roasted vegetables. Drizzle the balsamic vinegar over the top.

Nutrition Information (per serving):

Calories: 420 Total Fat: 18g Saturated Fat: 3g Cholesterol: 110mg Sodium: 420mg Total Carbohydrates: 21g Dietary Fiber: 7g Sugar: 8g Protein: 44g

MEDITERRANEAN GRILLED CHICKEN WITH LEMON AND HERB SAUCE

Preparation Time: 15 minutes
Cook Time: 20 minutes
Servings: 4

Ingredients:

- 4 boneless, skinless chicken breasts
- Salt and pepper, to taste
- 4 garlic cloves, minced
- 2 tablespoons olive oil
- 2 lemons, juiced
- 1/4 cup fresh parsley, chopped
- 1/4 cup fresh basil, chopped
- 1/4 cup fresh oregano, chopped
- 1/4 teaspoon red pepper flakes
- 2 tablespoons capers, drained

Instructions:

1. Season chicken breasts with salt and pepper on both sides.

2. Mix garlic, olive oil, lemon juice, parsley, basil, oregano, red pepper flakes, and capers in a small bowl.
3. Heat a large grill pan over medium-high heat and add chicken breasts. Cook for 6-7 minutes on each side until fully cooked.
4. Brush lemon and herb sauce over the chicken during the last 2 minutes of cooking.
5. Serve the grilled chicken hot with additional lemon and herb sauce on the side.

Nutrition Information (per serving):
Calories: 361 Total Fat: 22 g Saturated Fat: 4 g Cholesterol: 96 mg Sodium: 305 mg Total Carbohydrates: 7 g Dietary Fiber: 2 g Protein: 36 g

MEDITERRANEAN STUFFED BELL PEPPERS RECIPE

Preparation Time: 20 minutes
Cook Time: 40 minutes
Servings: 4

Ingredients:

- 4 large bell peppers (red, yellow, or green)
- 1 lb. ground turkey or chicken
- 1 cup cooked brown rice
- 1 cup chopped tomatoes
- 1/2 cup chopped onion
- 1/2 cup chopped red or yellow bell pepper
- 1/4 cup chopped fresh parsley
- 2 cloves garlic, minced
- 1/4 cup Kalamata olives, pitted and chopped
- 1/4 cup crumbled feta cheese

- Salt and pepper, to taste
- 1 tbsp. olive oil
- 1/2 cup chicken broth

Instructions:
1. Preheat oven to 375°F.
2. The bell peppers' tops should be removed, and the seeds and membranes should be removed.
3. Heat olive oil in a large pan over medium heat. Then, add chopped onion and red or yellow bell pepper and cook until the vegetables are tender, which may take about 5 minutes.
4. Add the ground turkey or chicken to the pan and cook until browned about 8-10 minutes.
5. Add the cooked brown rice, chopped tomatoes, parsley, garlic, Kalamata olives, salt, and pepper to the pan and combine.
6. Spoon the mixture into the bell peppers and place the peppers in a baking dish.
7. Pour the chicken broth around the peppers and cover the dish with foil.
8. Bake for 25 minutes, then remove the foil and bake for another 15 minutes or until the peppers are tender.
9. Sprinkle crumbled feta cheese over the peppers and serve.

Nutrition Information (per serving):
Calories: 360 Fat: 15g Saturated Fat: 5g Cholesterol: 70mg Sodium: 460mg Carbohydrates: 32g Fiber: 6g Sugar: 5g Protein: 26g

MEDITERRANEAN-STYLE GRILLED CHICKEN BREASTS

Preparation Time: 10 minutes

Cook Time: 20 minutes

Servings: 4

Ingredients:

- 4 boneless, skinless chicken breasts
- 1/4 cup extra-virgin olive oil
- 2 cloves garlic, minced
- 1 lemon, juiced
- 2 teaspoons dried oregano
- 1 teaspoon dried thyme
- Salt and pepper to taste

Instructions:

1. Whisk the olive oil, garlic, lemon juice, oregano, thyme, salt, and pepper in a large bowl.

2. Add the chicken breasts to the bowl and turn to coat in the marinade. Cover and refrigerate for at least 40 minutes or up to 4 hours.
3. Preheat your grill to medium-high heat.
4. Remove the chicken from the marinade and remove any additional marinade.
5. Place the chicken on the grill and cook for 6 to 8 minutes on each side until the internal temperature reaches 165°F.
6. Serve hot with your favorite Mediterranean sides, such as a fresh salad or grilled vegetables.

Nutrition Information (per serving):
Calories: 330 Fat: 22g Saturated Fat: 3g Cholesterol: 95mg Sodium: 140mg Carbohydrates: 2g Fiber: 1g Sugar: 0g Protein: 36g

MEDITERRANEAN-STYLE BAKED COD WITH TOMATOES, OLIVES, AND FETA

Preparation Time: 15 minutes
Cook Time: 26 minutes
Servings: 4

Ingredients:

- 4 cod fillets (about 6 ounces each)
- 1 tablespoon olive oil
- 1 medium onion, chopped
- 2 cloves garlic, minced
- 1 cup cherry tomatoes, halved
- 1/2 cup kalamata olives, pitted and chopped
- 1/4 teaspoon dried oregano
- Salt and pepper to taste
- 1/4 cup crumbled feta cheese

Instructions:

1. Preheat the oven to 400°F.
2. In a large oven-safe skillet, heat the olive oil over medium heat.

3. Add the onion and garlic, and cook until softened about 5 minutes.
4. Add the cherry tomatoes, olives, oregano, salt, and pepper, and cook for another 5 minutes.
5. Place the cod fillets on top of the tomato mixture in the skillet.
6. Bake in the oven for 15-20 minutes until the cod is cooked and flakes easily with a fork.
7. Sprinkle with the crumbled feta cheese, and serve with crusty bread or steamed vegetables.

Nutrition Information (per serving):
Calories: 250 Fat: 13 g Saturated Fat: 3 g Cholesterol: 60 mg Sodium: 550 mg Carbohydrates: 8 g Fiber: 2 g Protein: 26 g

MEDITERRANEAN-STYLE GRILLED SWORDFISH WITH HERB SALAD

Preparation Time: 15 minutes
Cook Time: 10 minutes
Servings: 4

Ingredients:

- 4 swordfish steaks, about 6 ounces each
- 4 teaspoons olive oil
- 1 teaspoon dried oregano
- Salt and freshly ground black pepper to taste
- 1 lemon, cut into wedges for garnish
- Herb Salad:
- 4 cups mixed greens
- 2 tablespoons chopped fresh parsley
- 2 tablespoons chopped fresh basil
- 2 tablespoons chopped fresh mint
- 2 tablespoons chopped fresh dill
- 2 tablespoons red wine vinegar

- 4 tablespoons olive oil
- Add salt and freshly ground black pepper according to your taste.

Instructions:
1. Preheat the grill to medium-high heat.
2. Combine the olive oil, oregano, salt, and pepper in a small bowl. Brush the swordfish steaks with the oil mixture.
3. Place the steaks on the grill and cook for about 5 minutes on each side until the fish is opaque and cooked through.
4. Combine the mixed greens, parsley, basil, mint, and dill in a large bowl to make the herb salad.
5. Whisk together the red wine vinegar and olive oil in a small bowl. Season with salt and pepper.
6. Pour the dressing over the herb salad and toss to coat.
7. Serve the swordfish steaks with the herb salad and lemon wedges on the side.

Nutrition Information per serving:
Calories: 327 Total Fat: 24 g Saturated Fat: 4 g Cholesterol: 76 mg Sodium: 74 mg Total Carbohydrates: 4 g Dietary Fiber: 2 g Protein: 26 g

MEDITERRANEAN GRILLED CHICKEN WIT..
CUCUMBER AND TOMATO SALAD

Preparation Time: 10 minutes
Cook Time: 20 minutes
Servings: 4

Ingredients:

- 4 boneless, skinless chicken breasts
- 1/4 cup olive oil
- 2 cloves garlic, minced
- 1 lemon, juiced
- 1 tsp dried oregano
- Salt and pepper, to taste
- 2 cucumbers, peeled and sliced
- 2 large tomatoes, sliced
- 1/4 cup crumbled feta cheese

- 2 tbsp red wine vinegar
- 1 tbsp chopped fresh basil

Instructions:
1. Whisk together olive oil, garlic, lemon juice, oregano, salt, and pepper in a large bowl.
2. Add the chicken breasts to the bowl and turn to coat.
3. Heat a grill to medium-high heat.
4. Grill the chicken for 5 minutes on each side or until fully cooked.
5. While the chicken is cooking, prepare the salad by tossing the sliced cucumbers and tomatoes together.
6. Whisk together the feta cheese, red wine vinegar, and basil in a small bowl.
7. Pour the dressing over the salad and mix it well.
8. Serve the grilled chicken with the cucumber and tomato salad on the side.

Nutrition Information (per serving):
Calories: 444 Fat: 27g Saturated Fat: 7g Carbohydrates: 9g Protein: 42g Fiber: 2g Sodium: 558mg

MEDITERRANEAN CHICKEN AND VEGETABLE BAKE

Preparation time: 15 minutes

Cook time: 40 minutes

Servings: 4

Ingredients:
- 4 boneless, skinless chicken breasts
- 1 red bell pepper, sliced
- 1 yellow bell pepper, sliced
- 1 zucchini, sliced
- 1 eggplant, sliced
- 1 onion, sliced
- 3 cloves of garlic, minced
- 1 can (14.5 oz) of diced tomatoes
- 1 tbsp. of tomato paste
- 2 tbsp. of olive oil
- 1 tsp. of dried oregano
- Salt and pepper to taste
- 1 cup of crumbled feta cheese

Instructions:

1. Preheat your oven to 400°F (200°C).
2. In a large skillet, heat 1 tbsp. Of olive oil over medium heat.
3. Add the sliced onion and minced garlic to the skillet and cook until the onion is soft and translucent about 5 minutes.
4. Add the sliced bell peppers, zucchini, and eggplant to the skillet and cook for 5 minutes.
5. Add the diced tomatoes and tomato paste to the skillet and stir to combine.
6. Add the dried oregano, salt, and pepper to the skillet and stir to combine.
7. Remove the skillet from heat and set aside.
8. In a separate large skillet, heat the remaining 1 tbsp. Of olive oil over medium-high heat.
9. Add the chicken breasts to the skillet and cook until browned on both sides, about 5 minutes per side.
10. Transfer the chicken breasts to a 9x13-inch baking dish.
11. Spoon the vegetable mixture over the chicken breasts in the baking dish.
12. Scatter the crumbled feta cheese on top of the vegetables.
13. Bake in the oven for 20-25 minutes or until the chicken is fully cooked and the cheese is melted and bubbly.
14. Serve hot, and enjoy!

Nutrition Information per serving (1/4 of recipe):

Calories: 350 Fat: 20g Saturated Fat: 6g Carbohydrates: 16g Protein: 28g Sodium: 550mg

MEDITERRANEAN BAKED COD WITH TOMATO AND OLIVE TOPPING

Preparation time: 15 minutes

Cook time: 26 minutes

Servings: 4

Ingredients:
- 4 cod fillets (6 ounces each)
- Salt and black pepper to taste
- 1 tablespoon extra-virgin olive oil
- 1 large onion, chopped
- 2 garlic cloves, minced
- 1 can (14.5 ounces) diced tomatoes, drained
- 1/2 cup kalamata olives, pitted and chopped
- 2 tablespoons chopped fresh basil
- 1 tablespoon chopped fresh oregano
- 1/2 cup crumbled feta cheese

Instructions:
1. Preheat oven to 400°F (200°C).
2. Season the cod fillets with salt and pepper.

3. Heat the olive oil in a large skillet over medium heat. Add the onion and garlic and cook until softened about 5 minutes.
4. Stir in the diced tomatoes, olives, basil, and oregano. Cook until the mixture is heated through, about 3 minutes.
5. Pour the mixture into a baking dish measuring 9 by 13 inches. Arrange the cod fillets on top of the tomato mixture.
6. Sprinkle the feta cheese over the top of the cod.
7. Bake the cod in the oven until fully cooked, and the cheese is melted and golden, about 20 to 25 minutes.
8. Serve the baked cod with steamed vegetables or a mixed greens salad.

Nutrition Info (per serving):
Calories: 320 Fat: 19g Saturated Fat: 5g Cholesterol: 65mg Sodium: 640mg Carbohydrates: 11g Fiber: 3g Protein: 27g

GRILLED SALMON WITH MEDITERRANEAN SALSA

Preparation Time: 20 minutes

Cook Time: 15 minutes

Servings: 4

Ingredients:

- 4 salmon fillets (6 oz each)
- 1 tsp salt
- 1 tsp black pepper
- 2 tbsp olive oil
- 1 cup cherry tomatoes, halved
- 1/2 cup chopped red onion
- 1/4 cup chopped fresh parsley
- 2 tbsp capers, rinsed and drained
- 2 tbsp lemon juice
- 1 tsp lemon zest
- 1/4 tsp red pepper flakes
- 2 cloves garlic, minced

139

Instructions:

1. Preheat the grill to medium-high heat. Sprinkle salt and pepper on both sides of the salmon fillets to season them.
2. Mix cherry tomatoes, red onion, parsley, capers, lemon juice, lemon zest, red pepper flakes, and garlic in a medium bowl.
3. Brush the salmon fillets with olive oil and place them on the grill. Cook 6-7 minutes on each side until the salmon is cooked and the skin is crispy.
4. Serve the salmon with Mediterranean salsa on top.

Nutrition Information (per serving):

Calories: 380 Fat: 26g Saturated Fat: 4g Cholesterol: 94mg Sodium: 790mg Carbohydrates: 6g Fiber: 2g Sugar: 3g Protein: 36g

GRILLED SALMON WITH OLIVE AND LEMON TAPENADE

Preparation time: 15 minutes

Cook time: 15 minutes

Servings: 4

Ingredients:

- 4 salmon fillets (6 oz each)
- Salt and pepper to taste
- 1/2 cup kalamata olives, pitted
- 1/4 cup fresh parsley, chopped
- 2 cloves garlic, minced
- 2 tbsp freshly squeezed lemon juice
- 2 tbsp extra-virgin olive oil

Instructions:

1. Preheat the grill to high heat.
2. Sprinkle salt and pepper over the salmon fillets to season them.
3. Combine the olives, parsley, garlic, lemon juice, and olive oil in a food processor. Pulse until well combined.

4. Place the salmon fillets on the grill and cook on each side for 5-7 minutes until the internal temperature reaches 145°F.
5. Serve the grilled salmon with a generous spoonful of olive and lemon tapenade on top.

Nutrition information (per serving):
Calories: 370 Fat: 27g Saturated fat: 4g Cholesterol: 93mg Sodium: 559mg Carbohydrates: 3g Fiber: 1g Sugar: 1g Protein: 31g

MEDITERRANEAN BAKED COD WITH TOMATO AND OLIVE RELISH

Preparation Time: 15 minutes
Cook Time: 26 minutes
Servings: 4

Ingredients:

- 4 cod fillets, about 6 ounces each
- 2 medium tomatoes, diced
- 1/2 cup pitted kalamata olives, chopped
- 2 tablespoons chopped fresh parsley
- 2 tablespoons capers, drained
- 1 tablespoon lemon juice
- 2 cloves garlic, minced
- Salt and black pepper, to taste
- Olive oil for drizzling

Instructions:

1. Preheat the oven to 400°F.
2. Line a baking sheet with parchment paper.

3. Combine the diced tomatoes, chopped olives, parsley, capers, lemon juice, and minced garlic in a medium bowl.
4. Add salt and pepper to taste the mixture and stir well.
5. Place the cod fillets on the prepared baking sheet.
6. Spoon the tomato, and olive relish over the cod fillets.
7. Drizzle the cod with a bit of olive oil.
8. Bake for 20-25 minutes until the cod is cooked and flaky.
9. Serve hot with a side of steamed vegetables or a mixed greens salad.

Nutrition Information (per serving):

Calories: 239 Fat: 10.3g Saturated Fat: 1.4g Carbohydrates: 7.6g Protein: 30.3g Sodium: 789mg

MEDITERRANEAN BAKED COD WITH TOMATO AND FETA

Preparation time: 10 minutes

Cook time: 20 minutes

Servings: 4

Ingredients:

- 4 cod fillets (about 6 ounces each)
- Salt and pepper, to taste
- 4 medium tomatoes, chopped
- 1/2 cup crumbled feta cheese
- 2 tablespoons olive oil
- 1/4 teaspoon dried oregano
- 2 cloves garlic, minced
- 1 lemon, sliced into rounds

Instructions:

1. Preheat the oven to 400°F (200°C).

2. Season the cod fillets with salt and pepper.
3. Combine the chopped tomatoes, crumbled feta, olive oil, oregano, and minced garlic in a large baking dish. Mix well.
4. Place the seasoned cod fillets on top of the tomato mixture.
5. Place a slice of lemon on each fillet after grilling.
6. Bake in the oven for 18-20 minutes or until the cod is fully cooked and flaky.
7. Serve hot with crusty bread, if desired.

Nutrition Information (per serving):
Calories: 324 Fat: 18.5g Saturated Fat: 5.5g Cholesterol: 84mg Sodium: 493mg Carbohydrates: 7.5g Fiber: 2g Sugar: 3.5g Protein: 36g

SIDE DISH
RECIPES

GRILLED FISH FILLET WITH PESTO SAUCE

Preparation time: 20 minutes

Cook time: 10 minutes

Servings: 4

Ingredients:

- 4 firm white fish fillets, about 6 oz each (such as cod or halibut)
- Salt and pepper, to taste
- Olive oil for brushing the fish
- 2 cups basil leaves, packed
- 1/2 cup freshly grated Parmesan cheese
- 1/2 cup pine nuts, toasted
- 4 garlic cloves, minced
- 1/2 cup extra-virgin olive oil
- Juice of 1 lemon
- Salt and pepper, to taste

Instructions:

1. Preheat your grill to high heat.
2. Brush olive oil over the fish fillets and season them with salt and pepper.
3. Combine the basil, Parmesan cheese, pine nuts, garlic, olive oil, lemon juice, salt, and pepper in a food processor. Blend until smooth.

4. Put the fish fillets on the grill for 5 to 6 minutes on each side. Make sure to season with salt and pepper and brush with olive oil before grilling.
5. Serve the grilled fish with a generous dollop of pesto sauce on top.

Nutrition information per serving:
Calories: 598 Total Fat: 48 g Saturated Fat: 9 g Cholesterol: 94 mg Sodium: 465 mg Total Carbohydrates: 7 g Dietary Fiber: 2 g Total Sugars: 2 g Protein: 40 g

GRILLED MEDITERRANEAN SALMON IN FOIL RECIPE

Preparation Time: 15 minutes
Cook Time: 15 minutes
Servings: 4

Ingredients:

- 4 salmon fillets (6 oz each)
- 4 tbsp pesto sauce
- 4 lemon slices
- Salt and pepper, to taste
- 4 tbsp olive oil
- 4 garlic cloves, minced
- 4 tbsp chopped fresh parsley
- 4 tbsp chopped fresh basil
- 4 tbsp chopped fresh dill

Instructions:

1. Preheat the grill to medium-high heat.
2. Cut 4 pieces of aluminum foil, large enough to wrap each salmon fillet.
3. Mix the olive oil, garlic, parsley, basil, and dill in a small bowl.

4. Sprinkle salt and pepper on each salmon fillet to season.
5. Place a salmon fillet in the center of each piece of foil.
6. Spoon 1 tablespoon of pesto sauce on top of each salmon fillet.
7. Put one slice of lemon on each piece of fish.
8. Divide the herb mixture evenly between each fillet.
9. Wrap each salmon fillet in the foil, sealing the edges tightly.
10. Place the wrapped salmon fillets on the grill and cook for 12-15 minutes until the salmon is fully cooked and the internal temperature reaches 145°F.
11. Serve hot with additional lemon wedges and fresh herbs, if desired.

Nutrition Information per serving (based on 4 oz salmon fillet):
Calories: 250 Protein: 28g Fat: 15g Carbohydrates: 2g Fiber: 0g Sodium: 120mg

GRILLED GARLIC AND HERB SHRIMP RECIPE

Preparation time: 10 minutes

Cook time: 10 minutes

Servings: 4

Ingredients:
- 1 lb large shrimp, peeled and deveined
- 2 tablespoons extra-virgin olive oil
- 4 garlic cloves, minced
- 2 tablespoons fresh parsley, chopped
- 2 tablespoons fresh basil, chopped
- 1 tablespoon fresh thyme, chopped
- 1 teaspoon salt
- 1/2 teaspoon black pepper
- 2 lemons, cut into wedges

Instructions:
1. Mix the olive oil, garlic, parsley, basil, thyme, salt, and pepper in a large bowl.
2. Place the shrimp into the bowl and stir to ensure uniform coverage with the blended herbs.
3. Preheat your grill to medium-high heat.

153

4. Place the shrimp on metal skewers or a piece of aluminum foil.
5. Grill the shrimp on each side for 2-3 minutes
6. Serve the grilled shrimp with lemon wedges.

Nutrition Information (per serving):

Calories: 200 Fat: 14g Protein: 20g Carbohydrates: 4g Fiber: 1g Sodium: 600mg

SPANISH MOROCCAN FISH

Preparation time: 15 minutes
Cook time: 20 minutes
Servings: 4

Ingredients:

- 4 (6-oz) firm white fish fillets, such as cod or halibut
- 2 tbsp olive oil
- 2 cloves garlic, minced
- 1 tsp ground cumin
- 1 tsp paprika
- 1/2 tsp ground coriander
- 1/4 tsp cayenne pepper
- Salt and pepper to taste
- 1 can (15 oz) of chickpeas, drained and washed
- 1 large red bell pepper, diced
- 1 large yellow onion, diced
- 1 can (14 oz) diced tomatoes
- 1 cup vegetable broth

- 1/4 cup chopped fresh cilantro leaves

Instructions:

1. Warm the olive oil in a sizable frying pan over medium heat.
2. Cook the garlic until it becomes fragrant, which should take about 1 minute.
3. Add the cumin, paprika, coriander, and cayenne pepper, and cook for another minute.
4. Sprinkle pepper and salt on the fish fillets for seasoning, then place them in the frying pan. Cook for approximately 2-3 minutes per side until the fish becomes translucent and easily flakes apart.
5. Remove the fish from the skillet and set aside.
6. Add chickpeas, bell pepper, and onion to the same skillet. Cook until the vegetables are soft.
7. Add the diced tomatoes and vegetable broth, and bring to a simmer.
8. Place the fish fillets back into the frying pan and spoon a portion of the sauce over each piece.
9. Place a lid on the frying pan and let it simmer for 5-10 minutes, allowing the vegetables to soften and the tastes to blend.
10. Serve the fish fillets with the sauce sprinkled with cilantro leaves.

Nutrition information per serving (based on 4 servings):

Calories: 330 Fat: 12g Carbohydrates: 25g Protein: 33g Sodium: 690mg Fiber: 8g

GRILLED OCTOPUS WITH OLIVE AND LEMON SALAD RECIPE

Preparation Time: 15 minutes
Cook Time: 15 minutes
Servings: 4

Ingredients:

- 1 pound fresh octopus, cleaned and chopped into 1-inch pieces
- 1/4 cup olive oil
- Salt and pepper, to taste
- 1 lemon, zested and juiced
- 1/4 cup pitted and diced kalamata olives
- 2 tablespoons capers, drained
- 1/2 red onion, thinly sliced
- 2 tablespoons chopped fresh parsley
- 4 cups mixed greens

Instructions:

1. In a sizable bowl, mix the octopus segments with olive oil, salt, black pepper, and grated lemon rind. Stir to ensure even coverage.

2. Heat a grill or grilling surface to a high temperature.
3. Grill the octopus pieces until charred and tender, about 2-3 minutes on each side.
4. Mix the lemon juice, kalamata olives, capers, red onion, and parsley in a separate bowl.
5. Serve the grilled octopus over a bed of mixed greens, topped with the olive and lemon salad.

Nutrition Information (per serving):
Calories: 333 Fat: 28 g Protein: 19 g Carbohydrates: 7 g Fiber: 2 g Sodium: 586 mg

FLOUNDER MEDITERRANEAN RECIPE

Preparation time: 10 minutes

Cook time: 15 minutes

Servings: 4

Ingredients:

- 4 flounder fillets (about 1 lb)
- Salt and pepper, to taste
- 1/4 cup all-purpose flour
- 2 tablespoons olive oil
- 1/2 cup cherry tomatoes, halved
- 1/2 cup Kalamata olives, pitted and sliced
- 2 cloves garlic, minced
- 2 tablespoons lemon juice
- 1/4 cup white wine
- 1/4 cup chopped fresh parsley
- 1/4 cup chopped fresh basil

Instructions:

1. Coat the flounder fillets with salt and pepper, then dip them in flour, removing any surplus.
2. Heat enough olive oil over medium heat in a large frying pan. Add the flounder fillets and cook on each side for 3 to 4 minutes or until golden brown. Remove the fillets from the skillet and set them aside.
3. Add the cherry tomatoes, Kalamata olives, and garlic to the same skillet and sauté for 2 to 3 minutes.
4. Mix the lemon juice, white wine, parsley, and basil in the saucepan and bring it to a boil. Then, turn down the heat to low.
5. Place the flounder back into the pan and cover it with the tomato and olive combination.
6. Cover the skillet and cook for another 2 to 3 minutes until the fish is fully cooked and the sauce has thickened slightly.
7. Serve the flounder with a generous spoonful of the tomato and olive mixture on top.

Nutrition information per serving:

Calories: 309 Fat: 18g Saturated Fat: 3g Cholesterol: 84mg Sodium: 719mg Carbohydrates: 12g Fiber: 2g Sugar: 3g Protein: 26g

BAKED HALIBUT STEAKS RECIPE

Preparation Time: 10 minutes
Cook Time: 25 minutes
Servings: 4

Ingredients:
- 4 (6-oz) halibut steaks
- 1/4 cup extra-virgin olive oil
- 4 garlic cloves, minced
- 1/4 teaspoon salt
- 1/4 teaspoon black pepper
- 1 lemon, sliced
- 1/4 cup chopped fresh parsley

Instructions:
1. Preheat oven to 400°F (200°C). Line a baking sheet with parchment paper.
2. Combine olive oil, garlic, salt, and pepper in a mixing bowl using a whisk.
3. Place the halibut steaks on the prepared baking sheet.
4. Brush the top of each steak with the olive oil mixture.
5. Gently place a lemon slice on top of each steak.

6. Bake the halibut steaks in the oven for 20-25 minutes until the flesh becomes tender and can be easily separated.
7. Sprinkle the chopped parsley over the steaks before serving.

Nutrition Information (per serving):

Calories: 277, Fat: 18g, Saturated Fat: 3g, Cholesterol: 68mg, Sodium: 257mg, Carbohydrates: 2g, Fiber: 1g, Sugar: 1g, Protein: 31g.

PALEO POACHED WHITEFISH IN TOMATO-FENNEL BROTH

Preparation time: 15 minutes

Cook time: 30 minutes

Servings: 4

Ingredients:

- 4 whitefish fillets (6-8 ounces each)
- 1 large fennel bulb, sliced
- 1 large onion, chopped
- 2 cloves of garlic, minced
- 2 cups of cherry tomatoes, halved
- 1 teaspoon of dried oregano
- 1/2 teaspoon of dried thyme
- 1/2 teaspoon of salt
- 1/4 teaspoon of black pepper
- 1/2 cup of chicken or fish stock
- 2 tablespoons of olive oil
- Fresh parsley, chopped, for garnish

Instructions:

1. Warm up the olive oil in a big saucepan over medium heat.
2. Add the sliced fennel, onion, and garlic to the saucepan and cook for 5-7 minutes until the vegetables are soft and fragrant.
3. Stir in the cherry tomatoes, oregano, thyme, salt, and pepper, and cook for 5 minutes.
4. Incorporate the chicken or fish stock into the mixture and bring it to a boil. After it, lower the heat and allow it to simmer for 10 minutes.
5. Place the whitefish fillets in the saucepan, spooning some tomato-fennel mixtures over the top.
6. With the saucepan covered, let the fish cook and become tender in the tomato-fennel broth for 10-15 minutes.
7. Serve the poached whitefish fillets with the tomato-fennel broth, garnished with fresh parsley.

Nutrition Information (per serving):

Calories: 330 Fat: 20g Saturated Fat: 3g Cholesterol: 95mg Sodium: 550mg Carbohydrates: 12g Fiber: 3g Sugar: 5g Protein: 29g

CALAMARI MARINARA RECIPE

Preparation Time: 15 minutes
Cook Time: 20 minutes
Servings: 4

Ingredients:
- 1-pound calamari rings
- 2 tablespoons olive oil
- 4 cloves garlic, minced
- 1 large onion, chopped
- 2 cans of crushed tomatoes (14.5 oz each)
- 1 teaspoon dried basil
- 1 teaspoon dried oregano
- Salt and pepper, to taste
- Fresh basil leaves for garnish

Instructions:
1. Rinse the calamari rings and pat them dry with paper towels.
2. Heat the olive oil in a large saucepan over medium heat.

3. Cook the minced garlic and chopped onion in the saucepan until fragrant and soft, usually taking 2 to 3 minutes.
4. Stir in the crushed tomatoes, dried basil, oregano, salt, and pepper.
5. Place a lid on the saucepan and gently allow the tomato sauce to cook for 10 minutes.
6. Uncover the saucepan and add the calamari rings to the tomato sauce. Stir gently to coat the rings with the sauce.
7. Cover the saucepan again and continue cooking for another 5-7 minutes or until the calamari is cooked.
8. Serve the Calamari Marinara over a bed of cooked pasta or with a slice of crusty bread for dipping.
9. Garnish with fresh basil leaves, if desired.

Nutrition Info (per serving):
Calories: 180 Fat: 9 g Saturated Fat: 1.5 g Cholesterol: 30 mg Sodium: 650 mg Carbohydrates: 13 g Fiber: 3 g Sugar: 6 g Protein: 12 g

MEDITERRANEAN PESTO-CRUSTED GROUPER

Preparation Time: 10 minutes

Cook Time: 15 minutes

Servings: 4

Ingredients:

- 4 (6 oz) grouper fillets
- 1/2 cup basil pesto
- 1/2 cup breadcrumbs
- 1/4 cup grated Parmesan cheese
- Salt and pepper, to taste
- Olive oil for brushing

Instructions:

1. Preheat oven to 400°F (200°C). Line a baking sheet with parchment paper.
2. Season the grouper fillets with salt and pepper.
3. Spread the basil pesto over the top of each fillet, making sure to cover it completely.
4. In a shallow dish, mix the breadcrumbs and grated Parmesan cheese.
5. Dip each pesto-covered fillet in the breadcrumb mixture, pressing it onto the fillet to ensure it sticks.

6. Arrange the fish pieces on the greased baking sheet and apply a thin layer of olive oil to each.
7. The dish should be cooked in the oven for approximately 15 minutes or until the crust turns golden and the fish is fully cooked.

Nutrition Information (per serving):
Calories: 400 Fat: 29 g Saturated Fat: 7 g Protein: 27 g Sodium: 722 mg Cholesterol: 83 mg

DESSERTS

CREMA CATALANA

Preparation Time: 15 minutes
Cook Time: 30 minutes
Servings: 4

Ingredients:

- 2 cups whole milk
- 1 cinnamon stick
- zest of 1 lemon
- zest of 1 orange
- 4 egg yolks
- 1/2 cup sugar
- 2 tablespoons cornstarch
- 1 tablespoon vanilla extract
- 2 tablespoons brandy or cognac (optional)

Instructions:

1. Heat the milk, cinnamon stick, lemon, and orange zest in a medium saucepan over medium heat until it just comes to a simmer.

2. Blend the egg yolks, sugar, and cornstarch in a big mixing bowl until the mixture becomes light and smooth.
3. Gradually add the hot milk mixture to the eggs while continuously whisking.
4. Heat the mixture in the saucepan again and continuously stir until it thickens, which should take around 5-7 minutes
5. Take the saucepan off the stove and mix in the vanilla essence and brandy (if desired).
6. Pour the mixture into 4 ramekins and refrigerate until set about 2 hours.
7. When ready to serve, sprinkle the top of each ramekin with sugar and caramelize with a kitchen torch or under a broiler.
8. Serve immediately.

Nutrition Information (per serving):
Calories: 255 Fat: 8 g Saturated Fat: 4 g Cholesterol: 199 mg Sodium: 42 mg Carbohydrates: 35 g Fiber: 1 g Sugar: 33 g Protein: 7 g

PASTÉIS DE NATA (PORTUGUESE CUSTARD TARTS)

Preparation Time: 40 minutes
Cook Time: 20 minutes
Servings: 12 tarts

Ingredients:
- 1 cup water
- 1 cup sugar
- 2 cinnamon sticks
- 1 lemon peel
- 4 egg yolks
- 1 cup whole milk
- 1/3 cup cornstarch
- 2 tablespoons unsalted butter
- 1 teaspoon vanilla extract
- 12 pre-baked tart shells
- Powdered sugar for dusting

Instructions:

1. Add the water, sugar, cinnamon sticks, and lemon peel in a medium saucepan. Cook the mixture over medium heat until the sugar dissolves, stirring occasionally.
2. Whisk the egg yolks, milk, and cornstarch in a separate bowl.
3. Once the sugar mixture has dissolved, remove the cinnamon sticks and lemon peel, and slowly add the egg yolk mixture to the saucepan, whisking constantly.
4. Keep whisking over medium heat until the mixture has thickened, about 5 minutes.
5. Remove the mixture from the heat and whisk the butter and vanilla extract.
6. Let the mixture cool for 10 minutes, then pour it into the pre-baked tart shells.
7. Bake the tarts at 350°F for 20 minutes or until they golden top.
8. Once the tarts have finished baking, allow them to cool down to room temperature before dusting them with powdered sugar and serving.

Nutrition Information per Serving (1 tart):

Calories: 250 Fat: 12 g Cholesterol: 110 mg Sodium: 60 mg Carbohydrates: 28 g Fiber: 1 g Protein: 4 g

IMQARET

Preparation time: 20 minutes
Cook time: 30 minutes
Servings: 12

Ingredients:

For the dough:

- 2 cups all-purpose flour
- 1/2 cup semolina flour
- 1/2 teaspoon salt
- 1/2 cup warm water
- 2 tablespoons olive oil

For the filling:

- 1 cup pitted dates
- 1/2 cup sugar
- 1/4 teaspoon ground cinnamon
- 1/4 teaspoon ground cloves
- 1/2 teaspoon orange zest
- 1/2 cup boiling water

Instructions:

1. To create the dough, mix the all-purpose flour, semolina flour, and salt in a big bowl.
2. In a separate bowl, mix the warm water and olive oil.
3. Gradually add the wet and dry ingredients and mix until a dough forms.
4. Work the dough for approximately 10 minutes until it is smooth and flexible.
5. After preparing the dough, cover it and allow it to rest for 15 minutes.
6. To make the filling, combine the dates, sugar, cinnamon, cloves, and orange zest in a saucepan.
7. Mix in the boiling water until a thick consistency is achieved.
8. Remove from heat and let it cool.
9. Divide the dough into 12 equal pieces.
10. Shape each piece of dough into a flattened disk of uniform thinness.
11. Place 1 tablespoon of the filling in the center of each circle.
12. Shape the dough around the filling to create a crescent shape.
13. Secure the edges of the dough to close the Imqaret.
14. Use enough oil in a deep frying pan to immerse the Imqaret.
15. Fry the Imqaret until golden brown on both sides, about 3-4 minutes.
16. Remove from heat and drain on a paper towel.
17. Serve the Imqaret warm or at room temperature.

Nutrition Information (per serving):

Calories: 244 Total Fat: 7 g Saturated Fat: 1 g Cholesterol: 0 mg Sodium: 134 mg Total Carbohydrates: 44 g Dietary Fiber: 2 g Sugar: 28 g Protein: 4 g

KREMNA REZINA

Preparation Time: 30 minutes
Cook Time: 40 minutes
Servings: 12

Ingredients:
- 1/2 cup unsalted butter, melted
- 1/2 cup sugar
- 4 large eggs
- 2 cups whole milk
- 1/2 teaspoon vanilla extract
- 1/4 teaspoon almond extract
- 1/2 teaspoon salt
- 1/2 teaspoon grated lemon zest
- 12 sheets of phyllo dough, thawed
- Confectioners' sugar for dusting

Instructions:
1. Preheat oven to 350°F. Grease a 9x13-inch baking dish.
2. Mix the melted butter and sugar in a large bowl until thoroughly blended.

3. Incorporate the eggs into the mixture one at a time, thoroughly mixing after adding each egg.
4. Add the milk, vanilla extract, almond extract, salt, and lemon zest, and whisk until well combined.
5. Place a single layer of phyllo dough in the bottom of the prepped baking dish, coating it slightly with the melted butter. Continue layering the phyllo sheets one by one, brushing each sheet with melted butter before placing the next one on top.
6. Pour the custard mixture over the phyllo dough into the baking dish.
7. Bake for 35-40 minutes until the top is golden brown, and the filling is set.
8. Let cool to room temperature. Dust with confectioners' sugar before serving.

Enjoy this rich and creamy Kremna Rezina as a sweet ending to your Mediterranean meal!

MADARICA

Preparation Time: 30 minutes
Cook Time: 20 minutes
Servings: 12 pieces

Ingredients:
- 2 cups all-purpose flour
- One-half cup of butter, at room temperature, that is unsalted.1/2 cup powdered sugar
- 1 egg yolk
- 1 tsp vanilla extract
- 1/2 tsp salt
- 1 cup almonds, toasted and ground
- 1/2 cup sugar
- 2 eggs
- 1 tsp lemon zest
- 2 tbsp lemon juice
- 1 tsp baking powder
- 1/4 tsp cinnamon

Instructions:
1. Mix the butter and powdered sugar in a large bowl until light and airy.

2. Add the egg yolk, vanilla extract, and salt, and mix until well combined.
3. Gradually add in the flour, and mix until a dough forms.
4. After wrapping the dough in plastic wrap, refrigerate it for 30 minutes before preheating the oven to 375°F (190°C).
5. Mix the almonds, sugar, eggs, lemon zest, lemon juice, baking powder, and cinnamon in a separate bowl.
6. Using a rolling pin, flatten the dough on a surface dusted with flour until it reaches a thickness of 1/8 inch.
7. Cut the dough into 3-inch circles, and place each circle in a muffin tin cup.
8. Spoon the almond mixture into the pastry shells, filling each cup about 3/4 full.
9. Put the tart in the oven and bake it for about 20 minutes, until the filling is firm and the crust is golden brown.
10. Serve either at a warm temperature or at room temperature, topped with a sprinkle of powdered sugar.

Nutrition information per serving: Calories:
305 Fat: 21g Carbohydrates: 26g Protein: 6g Sugar: 12g Sodium: 123mg

KANAFEH

Preparation time: 30 minutes
Cook time: 25 minutes
Servings: 4-6

Ingredients:

- 1 cup kataifi dough
- 1 cup unsalted butter, melted
- 1 cup granulated sugar
- 1 tsp. orange blossom water
- 1 tsp. rose water
- 1 cup heavy cream
- 2 cups shredded mozzarella cheese
- 1/2 cup chopped pistachios
- Vegetable oil for frying

Instructions:

1. Preheat oven to 350°F (175°C).
2. Combine the kataifi dough, melted butter, and 1/2 cup of sugar in a large bowl. Mix until well combined.

3. Grease a 9-inch (23 cm) baking dish with oil. Spread half of the kataifi mixture evenly over the bottom of the dish.
4. Whisk together the heavy cream, mozzarella cheese, and remaining sugar in a separate bowl until smooth. Spread the cheese mixture evenly over the kataifi in the dish.
5. Top the cheese mixture with the remaining kataifi mixture, pressing down gently to ensure the cheese is well covered.
6. Bake for 25 minutes until the kataifi is golden brown and crispy.
7. Heat the orange blossom and rose water over medium heat in a small saucepan until warm.
8. Remove the knife from the oven and drizzle with the warm syrup. Sprinkle with chopped pistachios and serve hot.

Enjoy your delicious and sweet Mediterranean-style Kanafeh!

HALVAH

Preparation Time: 10 minutes
Cook Time: 15 minutes
Servings: 16 (1/2 inch slices)

Ingredients:
- 2 cups tahini
- 1 1/2 cups granulated sugar
- 1/2 cup honey
- 2 tsp vanilla extract
- 1/2 tsp ground cinnamon
- 1/4 tsp ground cardamom
- 1/4 tsp salt
- 1/2 cup sliced almonds
- 1/2 cup sesame seeds

Instructions:
1. Whisk together the tahini, sugar, honey, vanilla extract, cinnamon, cardamom, and salt in a large saucepan over medium heat. Continuously stir the mixture until it becomes thick and begins to separate from the sides of the pan, which should take

approximately 15 minutes. Remove the pan from heat and stir in the almonds and sesame seeds.

2. Pour the mixture into a greased 9x9 inch square baking dish.
3. Once the halvah has cooled completely, wrap it up and place it in the refrigerator to chill for at least two hours or until it becomes solid. Once chilled, slice the halvah into 1/2-inch slices and serve.

Nutrition Information (per serving):

Calories: 259 Fat: 18g Saturated Fat: 2g Cholesterol: 0mg Sodium: 65mg Carbohydrates: 26g Fiber: 2g Sugar: 23g Protein: 5g

Made in United States
Orlando, FL
21 September 2023

37158420R00104